Copyright © Shar Moore, Michele Jones, Rebecca Bucci, Ruth Posterino, Genene Wilson, Linda del Amor, Min Melgar, Aldwyn Altuney, Louise L. Kallaway, Cathy Dimarchos, Kerri Speyers, Helen Froling, Ann Tomlinson, Savannah Falzon, Elissa Scott, Samantha Richards, Catherine Skiperdene, Shantelle Saiville, Jennifer Annette, Carol Aravena

First published in Australia in 2021 by Sharanis Publishing House

E | shar@sharmoore.com.au
W | www.sharmoore.com.au/linkshub
W | www.sphbooks.com
T | 1300 32 32 12

All rights reserved. No part of this book may be used or reproduced by any means, graphic, electronic, or mechanical, including photocopying, recording, taping or by any information storage retrieval system without the written permission of the copyright owner except in the case of brief quotations embodied in critical articles and reviews. Although the author and publisher have made every effort to ensure that the information in this book was correct at press time, the author and publisher do not assume and hereby disclaim any liability to any party for any loss, damage, or disruption caused by errors or omissions, whether such errors or omissions result from negligence, accident, or any other cause. This book is not intended as a substitute for the medical advice of physicians. The reader should regularly consult a physician in matters relating to his/her health and particularly with respect to any symptoms that may require diagnosis or medical attention.

Writer: Susannah Pask
Cover & Interior Design: Erica Anderson, Fidget Media
Cover Illustration: Sunny Gu
Proofreader: Rachel Francis

A catalogue record for this work is available from the National Library of Australia

Unlock Your Feminessence® Code/Shar Moore
Success/Self-help

ISBN: 978-0-6450811-4-5 (sc)
ISBN: 978-0-6450811-5-2 (e)

It all just started to make sense

It was like an important piece of the puzzle, made the entire picture visible.

You know the one I mean? When you place that piece into the puzzle and all of a sudden you can see the whole picture!

You see it was during the global pandemic (in 2020) that I had the greatest realisation I'd ever had. In truth, it was during one of the most difficult times of my life.

We published a women's empowerment magazine called YMag®, and for over eight years this magazine had been one of my main focuses. We profiled incredible women and shared their true purpose in life with the reader … their 'Y'.

And it no longer felt enough.

It felt like I was mid-sentence and just as the final page of the magazine turned over, right when I was about to share the most important thing with our readers, I stopped talking.

It felt like there was more depth required to this conversation. I needed to step up once more, (which was a very familiar feeling for me) and take my brand to the next level.

As I lay in bed one night, I sat bolt upright at around 3:00am and woke my husband Russ up. He was familiar with these 'midnight board meetings' of mine - when you are married for nearly 30 years, there isn't much you don't know about each other.

He flicked on the light as I felt a wave of words wash through my head, my heart and out of my mouth. I blurred my words together as they came rushing out and instead of saying 'I want to help women unleash their feminine essence', I said 'Feminessence®'.

He sat silent for a minute and I figured he was trying to catch up with the download I'd just thrown at him, but what he said next floored me.

He said 'Wow, that's a powerful word'. I had no idea what he was talking about and he said, 'You just said *Feminessence*®, I love it'.

And there it was. The gift I was given from my angels was right there in front of me. And I was not going to let it go. My lawyer had an email from me at 9:00am to trademark and secure this delightful name.

On March 8th 2021, we launched the Feminessence® Magazine, which is available online and also at leading Newsagents Australia wide. Nothing we do is traditional per se; our magazine only comes out twice a year and features the unique and inspirational stories of 14 powerful women. Each woman then shares an activity to help our readers to 'work on themselves' and to unlock their own Feminessence®.

And yes, we all have it inside us somewhere.

Our magazine brand is amazing but I wanted more. Funny that as my surname is 'Moore' and I am true to my name.

I wanted to reach more people and in a different way. I wanted to reach you through this book.

This book is your bible, your workbook, your inspiration and your best friend.

This book is a guide to how you too can unlock your own Feminessence® Code.

Our Feminessence® Code is unique to us. Which is Y I giggle a little when I hear women talk about competition ... no two divine women are the same, so how on earth can we be competing?

Take me as an example. Indian. Born in Thailand. Raised in Australia and from the age of 11 to 15, I was engaged to a man overseas. At fifteen-and-a-half my world changed when my beautiful Dad asked me if this is what 'I' wanted (refer to my TEDx talk for the full enchilada) and of course I said 'No!' Fast forward a tad to when I met the man of my choosing - we married, had two boys and adopted our little girl, and then travelled the world for eight years before settling down on the Gold Coast.

So when someone says we are in competition with each other, I beg to differ. How can someone compete with you when each of our stories are SO unique?

The short answer is ... 'You can't'.

The lens through which I see the world is different because of my story. So is yours.

My Feminessence® Code is unique because of how I unlocked it. So is yours.

So Beautiful, I invite you to sink yourself into your favourite spot and start turning some pages of this inspiring book.

Feel free to scroll through and read each chapter in any order you want - they are all individual and oh-so-powerful.

These women are just like you and me.

Read the stories.

Do the activities.

Connect with these ladies and share with them how (through their vulnerabilities and their willingness to share) it has helped you in some way - if it does, of course.

I truly hope that the pages of this book become well worn, that there are dog eared corners and yellow highlights throughout ... and that it changes your life, even a little.

Connect with our divine community on Facebook at the Feminessence® Movement and meet the women you have longed to connect with.

May you Unlock Your Feminessence® Code today and share with everyone you meet.

Big hugs to you Gorgeous and know this; you are not broken ... you are perfectly imperfect - as we all are.

UNLOCK YOUR FEMINESSENCE® CODE

CONTENTS

Michele Jones
Accessing Her Feminessence® to Expand Her World 1

Rebecca 'Bec' Bucci
From Tomboy to Queen of Hearts 15

Ruth Posterino
Helping Women Find Their True Personal Power 27

Genene Wilson
Helping You Take Control of Your Financial Future 41

Linda del Amor
Igniting a Divine Feminine Reset 55

Min Melgar
A Healing Journey to Find Wellness, Purpose and Abundance. 67

Aldwyn Altuney
Inspiring Gratitude and Good News.............................81

Louise L. Kallaway
Liberating Childhood and Adult Time Zones 97

Cathy Dimarchos
People are the Biggest Asset in Life and in Business; Starting
with You 109

Kerri Speyers
From Tomboy People Pleaser to Finding Feminessence® 121

Helen Froling
Finding Your Identity as a Woman 131

Ann Tomlinson
Using Feminine Know-How in a Male-Dominated Industry 143

Savannah Falzon
Personalised, Ethical and Respectful Elder Care 155

Elissa Scott
From Homeless to Millionaire.. 167

Samantha Richards
Teaching the Art of Confident Communication 179

Catherine Skiperdene
Standing Up for Women the World Over 191

Shantelle Saiville
Unstoppable. Unapologetic. 203

Jennifer Annette
Teaching Women How to Re-Capture Pleasure in Their Lives 213

Carol Aravena
Creating a Life You Love 227

MICHELE JONES

Founder and Creator LYBL™ - Live Your Best Life

Business and Life Empowerment Speaker, Educator, Author and Coach

Accessing her Feminessence® to expand her world

> *'Finding the parts of myself scattered everywhere and collecting them up as if piecing myself back together again, has been my life's deepest adventure'* — MJ

The year was 1986. I was 15 years old.

As I was dropped off at the door of some well-known and established four-star hotel located on the Gold Coast in Australia, I walked into the reception area, where I was greeted by a warm and friendly woman who was there to host me for the week.

She asked me to hand over my watch and directed me to a room that was downstairs from reception. It was set up with u-shaped desks along with block-out curtains drawn fully, so that not an inch of sunlight entered the room.

No sense of time. No sense of space. Placed inside another dimension. 'Where was the view of the ocean that had been displayed on their brochure', I wondered? Others joined the gathering one by one. Different ages, different genders, from all walks of life.

All *Excited. Fearful. Anticipating. Anxious.* Some feeling ready, others not even sure why they were there.

What unfolded over the course of the week would change my life … forever.

This seminar was the catalyst for me realising my innate ability and the connection or re-connection I found to be myself. My best self, which had appeared until that very moment to be laying hidden and dormant under the layers I had created to keep myself safe. Layers that in reality had only ended up hiding who I truly was. As my best self emerged from its slumber and took flight, I saw it release many unresourceful thoughts, which allowed me stop thinking I was a freak. I thought I was this freak because I seemed to see or think things that others didn't. I was no longer afraid to speak up and be me.

That wasn't the case when I first arrived there though.

As I sat in that five-day personal development and discovery seminar and was asked *'WHO AM I NEGATIVELY?'*, this was my response as recorded in my workbook:

'Growing up I was surrounded by hostility and hate. Not so much directed at me … but around me. (Unless of course you count being sexually abused by your stepdad for 12 years?) Hostility and hate expressed outwardly, often between my Mum and stepfather. So, I created a fantasy world for myself, full of nice things. There I could be number one, and people in that world – my world – would see me as such. In that world – my world – I was happy, and I belonged. Growing up I felt disillusioned, so I created a world of my own that was full of positive things to make life much happier and easier to face.'

'WHO AM I NEGATIVELY?'… I was 15 years of age, looking back and reflecting on my life when I was asked this question. When I entered that five-day seminar, I defined what I was seeking from this program:

Perspective.

Improvement.

Positive direction.

Creation.

Understanding.

I wanted to make a change in my life. In my thinking ... I was seeking a complete overhaul. I was at the end of my tether.

Lost.

Confused.

Frustrated.

Sad.

Hating.

Resentful.

Disillusioned.

Feeling ripped off by this thing called life ... already. I was looking for something new to grab hold of, something solid that I could depend upon. In fact, my life (as this young teenage girl) depended on it.

I entered the doors of this seminar with a deep understanding of who I was, but I certainly didn't like who that was and certainly cared a lot (at the time) about what others thought of me.

I was searching for change, but I didn't feel like I could do it alone. I had tried, I'd done okay, but I couldn't sustain it. I felt I could no longer stay on the outside looking in and at that moment in time, I felt like I had been running from my own reality.

I had been creating fantasy worlds in which to hang out and find enjoyment; day-dreaming up imaginary friends to enjoy life's adventures and journeys with; connecting with spirit guides and angels (treating them as old friends out there in the cosmos); escaping from my day-to-day reality.

I knew I had to go right in deep inside myself, where I could feel the truth (my soul's core essence), participate in it, connect with it on a deeper level. It was time to stop living in my fake existence of positivity and happiness, and to truly find myself again. I needed to answer the one burning question I was always asking myself, 'WHO AM I?'

It was time to participate in my own life, for real, not in my made-up yet universally connected world that I spent most of my days in. I had to find a way to function in my day-to-day life, rooted on earth.

I knew that there had to be more 'good' in people and in life than I could see at the time, and I had to find a way to see it or at least feel it. It was time for me to make contact with 'it' (the core of my soul's essence and reality) again, to connect with me again ... to my source. I didn't want to fool myself into thinking I had 'found' it any more. I no longer wanted a crutch to lean on; a bandage to cover the sore; a pill for the headache.

I was done living in a 24 hour-a-day vacuum. I wanted to deeply express the essence of life, right into the core of my being. I wanted to be truthful with myself and be okay with presenting this person to the world.

One of our seminar activities asked us to examine an image of a little girl who had a completely 'neutral' expression, and then answer the following questions:

'What was she saying to us?'

I said she was saying, 'HELP'.

What was she feeling within?

I said she was feeling 'DISILLUSIONED'.

What did she want?

I said she was wanting 'LOVE'.

All of my answers were projections of my own reality. I was focused solely on moving this little girl from neutral to being heard, felt and acknowledged. Within the little girl I saw me - wanting love, wanting myself to be an expression of love, wanting to give love.

I saw all of her, to the point of tears. Not the polite type of tears that roll slowly down your cheek, these were full blown, big-time snotty, uncontrollable tears. I sat there loudly sobbing, just staring at her. I wanted to hug her and tell her it would all be okay.

Deep down as I entered those doors and settled in, I knew the truth, however ugly or however beautiful was the only thing that could and would set me free.

I knew that even though I felt lost, it was all somehow perfectly as it was meant to be; that my personal human design (my own unique blueprint) would be exposed to me; that the universe had my back, it would come full circle and be known to me once more. I would reclaim that sense of what it felt like to be 'home' not only inside myself but also connected to the truth of my soul, and I would be able to fully express this with the world and to those around me. And more importantly, I would know that I was going to be okay.

I had always felt so incredibly connected to and held by the universe, yet my struggle was in feeling deeply held by other people as I found to enjoy my own company more than others.

At this point in time, I was yearning for other people to feel as connected to me as I felt to them, without them even knowing. I had to start by re-connecting with myself first - I wanted to listen and feel the truth deeply. It was time to rise above conditioning and circumstances.

I was willing to give up what I had been holding onto - my resentment, my pain, my hurt.

I had to stop living life as my 'false self' because, deep down I understood that my decisions and judgements were costing me emotionally. I needed to truly feel, to trust (others and myself). I had to peel away the layers, to dive in deeper to find me again.

It was time to take off my mask and free myself from the resentment and tyranny of my own illusion. It was time to create my own version of successful living – to focus on what that looked like to me, and to take complete ownership of and for my own life. I needed to live my very own version of my own best life. I had to learn how to step into the parts of me that I didn't know or had forgotten, like old friends becoming re-acquainted.

It was time to be free.

Little did I know, that this transformation and journey of self-discovery would go on to become the basis of some of my most impactful work to date, in my #1 best-selling book, *'Live Your Best Life'*. This book addresses some of the same questions presented to me at this 1986 retreat.

My own sense of Feminessence® started to rise within me at the seminar. It was an emergence within, that flooded my entire body. It whispered fiercely to me, telling me to start prioritising my heart over my mind and to start acting from the heart.

Up till then I had been living and loving life as a tom-boy - firmly rooted in my masculine and I didn't really know any other way. It had served me well. I had worked the land alongside my Stepdad and Mum as a farm hand - we laboured; preparing the land, sowing the seeds, tending to the crops and harvesting every Autumn. We also erected fence lines, herded, branded, wormed sheep and cattle, killed what we needed to live, took stock to the stockyard, fed the menagerie of animals and in general, I was one of the 'boys'. You name it, when it came to farming, I could do it ... or I would set my sights on it until I could!

My masculine had also kept me alive, safe, protected, driven, focused, alert and striving.

As a 15-year-old, I had been 'surviving' for so long; in fear, in my mind, switching between universal connection to a place and state of ego. I realised pretty quickly (as the layers of myself began to unravel) that I began to act from my own intrinsic intelligence and understanding rather than, giving my intellect the power of decision-making.

And there it was ... this connection I had known all too well but had seemingly lost. A universal and natural pulling, calling to me and urging me to live life fully expressed and not hold back.

Hello feminine side ... so nice of you to show up!

Being in our feminine-essence to me means living in alignment with our soul's purpose, which expands far beyond what we do for work. I'm not talking about male or female here, more the qualities of the expressions of the masculine and feminine energies that are present inside every being.

For me, living more deeply here in my feminine side, is about living with an open heart and listening to challenges deeply for all that they uncover about who I am. It's about answering the question *'How can I be the greatest service to the whole?'* and then setting about living that answer.

Thinking back, I always feel so grateful to my birth parents despite experiencing some of my life's greatest challenges growing up. My Mum didn't see any reason to throw expectations at me – and my Dad was, and still is, my greatest mentor. He was the reason I was at this five-day seminar in the first place. My life's trajectory as a 15-year-old wasn't looking that pretty, and he held the wisdom to direct me there.

It's fair to say, that despite the *'bad stuff'* that happened to me as a kid; being sexually abused for 12 years and the years that have followed on my path to healing, taking (what we thought were) my last breaths and dying from an asthma attack when I was 15 then waking up two weeks later in ICU, living my life with endometriosis from the age of 17, being diagnosed with cervical cancer at 23 (to name just a few) were the gifts that set me up for a life without limits. This brought me an understanding of the beauty in duality of contrast and an awareness of when I was living my life misaligned to my unique human design.

It is up to each of us as empowered individuals to claim, own and account for our slice of the suffering in life. Suffering is a part of humanity. The more 'real' we get with our wound mechanisms, our traumas, our contractions and our defence mechanisms, the more we are able to show up in an empowered way, because we are not denying any part of our reality.

We are actually embracing, owning and accounting for all that is us.

Finding the parts of myself scattered everywhere and then with each new challenge, collecting them up as if piecing myself back together again, has been my life's deepest adventure. Because of this, I've always gone after everything I've ever truly desired (very rarely leaving any stones unturned) to live a rich, deep and fully expressed life.

The expression of my business naturally became an extension of myself and my life experiences, along with being a dedication to my craft.

For You Corporation Pty Ltd was born in 2006 but it took over 20 years for me to fully birth it and to give it life … change can happen in an instant, and it did, but the transition of embodiment surrounding the truth takes time to nurture.

LYBL, Live Your Best Life started as the company's tagline before morphing into a life force of its own. It all started from a concept which was destined to transform the lives of thousands of people over the years, created inside me as a 15-year-old at the very seminar mentioned earlier.

I set about developing a series of seminar experiences and a variety of workshops, programs and offerings. Each is designed to give the individual an insight into their own unique truth; an understanding of what is needed to accept responsibility for oneself on this planet. Through these seminars, our programs and mentorship, LYBL birthed itself and took flight. It has continued to evolve and gain its own lifeforce, providing a source of insight and awareness for a wide variety of people from all walks of life.

Our programs and offerings recognise and realise the most important thing - YOU! We understand, that there are two main ingredients, you and your life. When you start with you, the other components that make up your life, simply fall into place. You become your own ultimate life creator.

Career, Business, Relationships, Personal Growth and Development, Finances, Wealth, Fun, Recreation, Health, Wellbeing, Physical Environment, Spirit and Soul – these areas ALL make up your LIFE, along with anything else you use to define your life.

So, although, I started in this space working with Business Owners and Entrepreneurs, our work soon flourished to reach anyone who knew there was more to the life they were living.

My team and I are not psychologists or psychiatrists, we are qualified as trainers, coaches and consultants amidst other holistic modalities. We are ordinary people from varied backgrounds who (for more than 15 years) have guided thousands of people through these various experiences – empowering them to be seen, heard, felt and celebrated.

What we provide cannot be a cookie cutter or one size fits all approach. We are not here to tell you how it should be for you. However, we are here to guide you through your own experience and to enable you to re-evaluate your LIFE. At the very least, we help you to make some sense out of your unique being and your direct purpose - so you can break free of the past and arrive at a place where you are living your best life.

As I write this chapter, I am speaking to YOU, to guide you to a better understanding of yourself and to empower you to broaden your own world view - regardless of how challenging that is. This is what living your best life is all about – walking in the duality of contrast of your shadows towards the light.

We are human beings, after all. We all face these situations to varying degrees. Most human beings feel totally helpless in their lives at different points along the way. There are times when we all feel like everything is out of control and nothing is in our control.

We spend all our time trying to control our lives, trying to pretend we're something that we're not, trying to pretend that we're living lives that we care about, and the reality is that we usually don't. We feel alone when behind closed doors.

And you don't have to be Einstein to connect the dots. At least one-third of our global population are now on *'happy'* pills. We are living within a depressed society.

Most human beings know there is more to life, but they just have nothing left in the tank, or have given up trying to connect with it - even people who are self-acclaimed personal development junkies like me! Most are all still seeking … seeking the answers to who they truly are, along with their own best life, filled with meaning, value, contribution and growth.

Our aim at LYBL is to connect each of the individuals, we're privileged enough to interact with, with their own uniqueness. Every single one of us has the capacity to be our own original masterpiece. The core of our work is guiding you directly to who you truly are as YOU.

LYBL is simply a path for you to use to explore yourself in your own self-discovery mission. We're about you digging with focus (like an archaeological dig), excavating and dusting off your own best life blueprint - to bring the diversity of your soul's uniqueness into a conscious world. We are here for you as your guide, you simply step into our environments, take the basic tools, connect with how they can serve you and express yourself through them.

You must do it your way. Take your time, there is no need to rush - unless you feel the need to go fast. We have one vision, for you to live YOUR best life. Nothing more.

We believe and as most would say … Living YOUR best life IS everything. We believe it IS your most important journey as a human being.

We look forward to joining you as your LYBL guides, on your own best life path and on your mission to self-discovery. It is here that you will learn that you already hold all the keys. You are the one who decides when it's time to turn them.

Unapologetically.

Confidently.

Gracefully.

We're here for YOU.

This is YOUR life.

Success to me is self-love. It is first an inside job – MJ

MICHELE JONES
Live Your Best Life

M: 0414 983 574
E: michele@lybl.com.au
W: www.lybl.com.au

Michele believes she was put on this planet to guide you to your own empowerment, so you can live your best life. She will assist you to grow your life or business creatively and consciously through understanding yourself at an even deeper level, so you can bring your soul's essence to life.

Michele knows YOU are a powerfully creative being and that your life matters.

That's because YOU matter.

If you run your own business, you will know that it emerges from your heart and that it has its own genius and purpose - it is tied to you with golden threads.

When you create your world in partnership with its soul, you enter a field of profound growth and miracles can occur.

As you go about your life, you and your business become a beacon of light, clarity and joy, irresistible to others (to clients, to customers, allies and enthusiasts who love what you do) who are all there saying 'YES' to the adventure of everything you do or offer.

Those you serve or interact with, know you do this for their deepest desires, which allows them to unfold their own souls - helping to shape prosperity and freedom for everyone.

For the past 28 years Michele has guided, trained, coached, consulted and mentored thousands of people in life and business. All of whom are committed to building a better world and making a difference.

Michele's strengths are in helping them to lead with soul and then follow with strategy.

She doesn't believe in marketing blueprints or 'one-size-fits-all' strategies that leave people more disillusioned, empty, dissatisfied and off course.

Together with Michele you will marry what you're building for your life or business with why and how you're building it - because that's where the magic is. You will uncover the genius that is uniquely yours, so you can design, create and live a life you love. A life that flows from your heart and powerfully serves the people you care about most.

She does this through one-on-one mentoring, strategic consulting, team workshops and forums, self-study programs, transformational retreats and more.

Michele looks forward to embarking on this journey together with you.

OFFER:

As a Feminessence® VIP, please connect with us today in order to embark on your own Live Your Best Life adventure - designing, creating and living your best life.

This is our invitation to contact us via email (at connect@lybl.com.au) and request your complimentary copy of our 30 page 'Release Your Life Blocks & Live Your Best Life' workbook (valued at $397).

And please feel free to also head on over to our website and subscribe to the Live Your Best Life community newsletter, as your welcome aboard emails are packed with loads of LYBL Goodies. You'll find us at
www.lybl.com.au

Don't delay another day to live the life you dream of, start living your best life today.

We look forward to joining you on your journey.

Photography © Scott Harrison – Daily Salt

Activity

1. Reflecting on duality of contrast - Who are you negatively? Who are you positively?

____

____

____

____

2. How can you be of greatest service to the world?

____

____

____

____

3. What does 'living your best life' mean to you?

____

____

____

____

4. What is holding you back?

____

____

____

____

5. What decisions do you need to make and what conversations do you need to have?

____

____

____

____

14

From tomboy to
Queen of Hearts

> *'Whilst it would have been much easier to be a victim of my past, I chose to become a survivor'* – RB

The road less travelled describes my life journey.

I grew up in a small coal mining town in NSW, raised by a single mother and my grandparents who were very traditional. Although we lived in difficult financial times, we always had room for laughter; a glass half full attitude to life's most difficult situations would serve me well into the future and help me overcome personal challenges related to childhood trauma.

I was never your typical little princess as a youngster; in fact, I wished I had been born a boy because I preferred riding my BMX with my shirt off with all the boys, rather than playing Barbies with the girls. I was a tomboy through and through, so it was often difficult to get me to look at a dress, let alone wear one. I was a little adventurer, and an opinionated one at that. I believe I was born a feminist; I had a gypsy spirit and a sense for justice when it came to gender equality. A deep spiritual knowledge also came through with my heritage link to my Native American roots, and the 'Lenape Wolf Tribe' who believe that we are all connected and part of a much a larger plan. As a young girl I never felt as though I fitted in; I was slightly awkward and very shy, and I was often bullied at school by the 'cool girls'.

I was a four-eyed, chubby, shy tomboy that was dealing with issues of abuse, learning to keep secrets that would convince me for many years into adulthood not to trust. I was ashamed of my sexuality, even scared of it. Being feminine had invited the worst kind of attention and I wanted to run far, far away from it. The expectation was to be a 'good girl' and that meant keeping quiet. I really had no idea that I was any different from the other girls and I believed that my reality must be 'normal'. Coming into my teenage years and womanhood, I started to realise that I was, in fact different to 'most' girls.

The Survivor

Whilst it would have been much easier to be a victim of my past, I chose to become a survivor. This laid the foundations for the choices I would make throughout my life, ultimately leading me to become a sex advocate; a voice for those we may judge due to their uniqueness, a voice for women standing in their divine femininity, embracing the light and dark of all that makes them whole. I discovered my essential power as a woman when I realised I could step out of the shame and into the light of humility and reverence. I could take my experiences and transform them into tools for growth and positivity. I could lead the way out of the darkness for so many who like me had not found the path back to their true nature, their true higher self. Once I freed myself from the cage I had created, the whole universe opened up. I was finally in flow, and I stopped pushing against what I could not change. I finally embraced all my curves and all my edges. I learnt to listen to what my environment was trying to show me. I stepped into my life purpose fully and completely. I let go of 'other people's' opinions, judgements and insecurities surrounding the work I was put here to complete. When you are 'on purpose' the journey is no longer just about you, it's about your contribution too humanity and how you can ease suffering for others by allowing them to become more of who they really are. Doing the work of breaking down prejudice around sexuality, taboos, kinks, fetishes, relationship dynamics, fantasies, deeper sexual expression and stepping into the divine masculine and feminine has become my life's work.

I feel I was always destined to do Goddess work. I was born on Friday the 13th (the Day of the Goddess), a time to worship the divine feminine in us all and a time to release the old (death) and step into the new (rebirth). The purpose in my work is to bring balance to the masculine and feminine within an individual and within a coupling union, guiding these connections to a place where each person can hold space for another and feel for the first time that they can be fully seen, without judgement or ridicule. That was the turning point for me, I am a Goddess, raw, real, beautiful – just like every other woman – and that is the essence of this divine femininity running through our veins. We can recreate ourselves. We can choose to believe that it is our birthright to be honoured in this way, as the great creators of life and the sacred vessel in which birth transcends; the sensual lover, the temptress, holding the key to the doorway of creation. Sexuality is defined as the way in which people experience and express themselves sexually, however I believe it is the foundation to everything in existence. It is the driving force behind continuous expansion within the individual and the community at large. Love and physical touch are what keeps us connected to one another.

Awakening

I came to realise my own innate ability to connect to my best feminine self by letting go of the fear that had kept my yearnings captive for far too long. I wanted to be real and completely raw with myself and the people in my life. I wanted to experience transparency in my relationships in ways that allowed me the freedom to be exactly who I am – to take back the veil, remove the mask and live an intimate, brutally honest human experience. I simply could not pretend that I was OK with the average life, by having an average relationship. I wanted to wake up. I am an explorer of new frontiers, pushing the boundaries of what we think is possible, or what we have been led to believe is true. The time had come to step wholeheartedly into the essence of the divine Goddess, to embrace every version of the self that had been created, combining them

to become as 'one' in unity to be in service to others; to lead a sexual revolution in which women's sexual desires would be finally celebrated, even adored, not weakened by insecurities, oppression, and patriarchal indoctrination.

Time to take on the modern persona of Sex Goddess, Ancestress or Queen, because the 'muse' exists in every woman, mysterious, beautiful and seductive. She is the archetype that inspires art and literature, and her charm and enigma ensnare her lovers. She is the siren we all long to embrace and become. She is taboo, a desired negative – men can lust after her, men can desire her BUT we are not supposed to BE her. Why? This was the question that probed my feminist nature, for if men adore extremely intelligent, attractive, and seductive woman, why should they not then shower her goddess self with her heart's desires? We are yearning to experience our sexuality in its purest form yet denying ourselves the freedom to express it at the same time. Modern femininity is waking up, at last. It is the second wave of transformation in relationship dynamics which embraces the masculine and feminine within each of us, and the balance is in becoming a whole unit, both together and apart.

When I discovered the freedom and relief of this epiphany, I could finally step into my true femme fatal self, without apology, without shame, without guilt, without fear of judgment. I wanted that for every woman.

Facing Judgement

And yes, I face other people's narrow-minded judgement and public opinion. When I tell people, I am a sexologist and tantric educator, I get one of two reactions – excitement or shock horror. This is usually determined by their strict upbringing or religious bias. Religion has, after all, been a major oppressor of female empowerment and sexual expression. Over the centuries, women have been persecuted for being born with the only organ whose sole purpose in the human body is to produce pleasure - the clitoris. Women have been called witches and burned alive for our 'promiscuous ways'; we've had our clitorises mutilated to impede our pleasure and been told to water down our sex appeal because when a man takes a woman's virtue without permission, she must have 'done something to deserve it'. Speaking out can create controversy and draw unwanted attention from those challenged by the emergence of a 20th century sexual liberal ideology that is opening the avenues of love and 'normalcy'.

I have no judgment around what is right or wrong for a couple or an individual walking their sexual path and I believe that their sexual journey is intrinsically connected to their spiritual journey. These two expressions influence an individual's level of comfort and satisfaction both within themselves and in their interactions with others. I specialise in areas of taboo which can attract all types of judgments, even personal attacks on my character. I have come to understand that this is due to a lack of education and understanding, so it no longer affects me. I have faced much opposition; anyone who is brave enough to stand naked in the crowd is going to get some pushback. The key is to learn how to turn negativity into positive growth. Now when I am challenged by a judgement or negative comments, I address it head on, from an educational viewpoint. My family has been very supportive, and they encourage my activism around conscious sexuality, which gives me the fortitude to keep moving forward. Everything is surmountable; sometimes we just need to think outside the 'box'.

What is Feminessence®?

What is the essence of being a woman? I think it is about self-acceptance. To know herself, have self-confidence without arrogance and complete acceptance of who she is allows for her true essence to fully bloom, unrestricted by the judgement or views of others. Femininity encapsulates the delicate balance between the masculine and the feminine, and the combination of the two is quite literally, life giving. Whole-hearted, bare-chested femininity is the outward projection of abundance, love, passion, sexual expression, and the power both to lead and to yield.

'Love the skin you are in', truly, that is essence in a nutshell. Men and women both have the capacity to express feminine and masculine traits; men provide and protect, women nurture and create. Yes, there are some obvious physical differences, but I innately believe men and women are more closely aligned than we realise.

The Juggler and the Octopus

Although we live in an era of so-called sexual equality, women still find themselves in a balancing act of juggling children, partners and multiple businesses. It is an ongoing challenge - and one that requires adaptability. Administration and organisation are not my strong suits. You really have no choice but to learn new skills, find new solutions to problems that need solving and not beat yourself up when you make mistakes. You will make mistakes in both your business and personal life balance. My advice is to accept that. I was so hard on myself in the beginning. I thought the world was ending if I failed at completing everything perfectly. Then you start to realise that nothing is ever completely perfect or will remain that way. Life is fluid.

I started life like a tree that eventually morphed into an octopus. The octopus has nine brains – one central brain and one in each of its eight arms, allowing each arm to work independently of one another, yet working together with the same goal. They are also able to change colour and texture in the blink of an eye making them highly adaptable to sudden changes in their environment. Like the octopus, I am dedicated to adapting to whatever is necessary to sustain my brood, and as their sole carer, make the necessary sacrifices. Ultimately there are going to be some disappointments and some moments we may miss. Life is difficult. Juggling daily commitments requires focus and prioritising what is most important to you. Success requires work, and sometimes short-term personal gain must be traded for the long-term benefit.

Women in Business

How do women contribute effectively and successfully in business?

Unconscious gender bias pervades every aspect of life and even more so in the workplace. This is part of the reason I became a sexologist – to liberate the unconscious and bring it into the conscious. Women need to lean on their strengths, not reinvent themselves in the masculine in order to compete. NO – you are already a super-hero, a female super-hero, you are not Clark Kent but Lois Lane. Let's think about who actually held the power in that working relationship! As women we know what men want. Right? Powerful, successful, confident women are some of the sexiest and most feminine woman in the world. They have embraced their femininity to its fullest capacity, and they use it to their fullest potential. Don't try to become a man, be a woman. I say, become an expert in your chosen field; having authority of your subject matter is your trump card.

This is an exciting time to be a woman. Many sacrifices made by those who have come before you have created the opportunities we now see today. Your passion will lead you to victory. I acknowledge now that I am not really in competition with my male counterpart, rather if I open my perspective and see that I am the yin to his yang, then I have restored the delicate balance that opens a space of combined unity towards a common goal.

My Life's Work

In my business, I am a certified Sexologist or some people refer to me as a 'Sexpert'. I am also an educator of the Tantric teachings, White Tigress Teachings (ancient Chinese concubine techniques) and the facilitator of sexuality workshops for couples and singles at Gspot Sex Therapy Down Under. I am the 'Love Doctor, and I specialise in relationship Taboos such as Kink, BDSM, Fetish and Dominatrix play. I assist couples with the navigation of open relationships, polyamory, and the swinging lifestyle. I also work with sexual rehabilitation of paraplegics, sexual /penal dysfunction and premature ejaculation. As a sex advocate, I am passionate about guiding clients through how to navigate their sexual relationships, desires and fantasies. Infidelity in couplings can largely be attributed to the lack of sexual interaction or the inability to express sexual desires openly to one another.

There can be many reasons why a coupling expires. My therapy and couples retreats focus is on what is happening in the bedroom and how it is translating into daily life.

When there is trouble in paradise, it usually rears its ugly head under the bed sheets. I teach the 'chemistry of connection' to couples internationally, in person and online. We are sexual creatures who crave human touch and the feeling of being adored by someone. Of course, it is not just about having great sex and long-lasting orgasms, ALTHOUGH they bare high on the priority list for most of us if we are being perfectly honest. It is also about learning new ways to communicate needs or improve or change current rituals. Changing old habits and patterns of relating, rediscovering erogenous zones and finding new ones, overcoming blocks to experiencing ecstasy and full body orgasms, sustained erections, finding the G Spot and what to do with it, erotic and sensual massage coaching are just a few areas of expertise which are important aspects of my work. There is a fundamental cornerstone to all relationships and that is - connection. It is about truly connecting with your lover on a deep soul level. Allowing the veil of who we pretend to be or think we have to be to fall away, so we can stand naked and raw, whilst they learn to hold the space for us to simply be and be present. This is the most powerful gift of all. To honour the pure beauty of the human spirit is the sexiest experience on the planet. Opening of the heart, soul and mind is the only road to full body orgasm.

What motivates me every day is witnessing a couple experiencing a deeper connection, discovering ways in which they can explore pleasure and ultimately falling in love all over again. More than that, as individuals, couples or singles, my clients experience deep feelings of unconditional love for themselves and towards others. It is like any journey we take to self- master; some choose a church; others enter the temple of love. The most powerful and most healing energy on the planet is sexual. If we can learn to understand it, we will no longer fear it and then we can cultivate it for greatness. That is when the magic happens. Creating miracle and magic – that is my Y!

Happy Couples

Did you know that close to 80 percent of woman do not orgasm during intercourse? Everyone wants to improve their sex life, in one way or another and I'm proud to say that I have managed to lead many women to discover their 'cliteracy' and many men to discover the GSpot adventure. It has been extremely rewarding both personally and from an educational perspective. I love to see happy couples, especially ones with newborns. A heart-warming success story for one client that did make my eyes well a little occurred earlier this year. Premature ejaculation and erectile dysfunction effects more men in 2020 than ever before. Having a baby was high on the priority list for this particular couple (whom we will call Jim and Karen). Jim discovered his ED concern was making it very difficult to conceive their first child and after a year of trying the 'old- fashioned' way, it seemed that artificial insemination was the only solution. Jim didn't feel satisfied with that option and felt as though he was failing as a man and as a husband, so he decided to try one last option - therapy with a sexologist. Over the next six months I consulted with Jim and his wife and gave them ways to prolong erections through techniques, practice and breathing exercises. It was an absolute joy to open a Thank-You card with a very special image attached of their eight-week ultrasound. By owning his dysfunction and sharing this with his wife they forged a deep bond, both expressed a stronger connection with each other than before. GSpot Sex Therapy Down Under had its first baby born in October!

Another area of great success is teaching women how to step fully into their relationship with their 'internal temple' (as I like to call it). External orgasms have often been mistaken for GSpot and internal orgasms. The study of the vulva and internally mapping of the vagina can lead to more fulfilling and intense orgasms for women. There is nothing more powerful than a woman letting go of her inhibitions and fully experiencing pleasure. I love sending sexually confident women home to their partners!

My Y

We are here, in essence, to experience being alive, to deep dive into the entire human experience and kaleidoscope through the full range of emotions in all their shades of complexity. Sexual exploration and the practice of Tantra is the vehicle I use to guide you there, to the place in which you shall know yourself and become the weaver of your own destiny. To prepare the heart to be open and the mind ready to receive the gift of pleasure and unconditional love. That is ultimately what I do.

That is my Y.

REBECCA 'BEC' BUCCI

M: 0491 030 499
E: info@gspotaustralia.com.au
W: www.gspotaustralia.com.au

GSpot's Love Doctor 'Lady Love', Rebecca Bucci, began her wellness journey 22 years ago when she open her first holistic wellness centre in Melbourne Australia.

With a passion for living her purpose and inspiring others to do the same, her work eventually lead her to the topic of sexual health, exploration and pleasure states. Her focus is on encouraging women and men to fully explore their sexual self - as a pursuit of self-development and personal discovery.

Certified as both a Sexologist and a Clinical Sexuality Coach, Rebecca specialises in all areas of taboo, couples retreats and sexuality workshops. She is the founder of GSpot Sex Therapy Down Under and the Director of Samaya Temple Of Tantra Teachings.

Rebecca is a certified Reiki Master and the Director of COBRA Self Defence Systems Western Australia. She runs her workshops and retreats here in Australia and internationally. In addition, she is the Ambassador for Noir Handmade Australia - an exclusive lingerie range that compliments her own 'Queen of Hearts' Lady Love fashion label - designed by Australian fashion designer Mauricio Alpizar. Rebecca's podcast series 'Killer Queens' - 'Let's get cliterate' is available on most audio platforms.

OFFER:

**Receive a 10% discount
on any online purchases when you use "Lady Love" code at**
www.gspotaustralia.com.au or www.samaya.com.au

Photography © Abbey Madison Body and Soul Boudoir photography

Activity

Orgasms are lets face it good for us, they help reduce stress, improve your drive and in general make us feel good about ourselves.

However for many of us the conversation around the quality and type of orgasm we would like to experience is avoided. For many women orgasms, even more so those achieved through penetration can be elusive let alone having an success locating the G spot.

Only about 18 percent of women can achieve orgasm via penetration alone (meaning no other external stimulation), so if you fall into this category, you are within the majority - Breathe out.

So how do we find the G spot? Its important to remember that the G spot is not a specific piece of anatomy but rather forms part of your clitoral network. So the man in the boat or small external pea is really just the tip of the iceberg of your clitoris.

So this may take some practise and it's important to be patient, you may also experience the sensation of feeling like you want to urinate, which is really the female form of ejaculation.

The best way to start exploring your G spot is to begin by using two fingers inserted into the vagina fingerprints facing upward towards the belly button and gently rubbing the upper wall in a home here fashion.

You can generally find that the most pleasurable area is located underneath your mound of venus, the soft mound just above your pubic bone. You can externally stimulate the clitoris and place some pressure on the mound of venus to intensify your orgasm.

Not all women will find pleasure from G spot stimulation and thats perfectly normal. Once you have found your G spot you can then explore the following best sex positions that will stimulate the G spot during intercourse.

I recommend the following with the first being the most successful - Doggy Style which also allows for external stimulation of the clitoris - Cowgirl - using a rythmic circular motion of back and forth - Closed missionary position - ladies bring legs together to create a firmer squeeze.

Let go of any expectations of an outcome and allow yourself and your body to respond organically. Above all - have fun with your person and remember to enjoy the exploration of each other as an experience of playfulness and an opportunity to deepen your connection.

RUTH POSTERINO

Founder – Personal Leadership Academy

Helping women find their true personal power

> *'The true voice of the lesson lies in the reckoning'* – RP

So, what has my life really been about?

I came out of complex trauma and survived. Then thrived. It was a childhood that was extreme, challenging, difficult, tough… and I emerged on the other side. Steering myself again and again away from the face of hopelessness, helplessness and haplessness. Even though the promise of death kept drawing me in, I kept choosing life. Something inside me said "Keep asking, keep moving, keep questioning. There is something on the other side of this".

At times though, I didn't even think I'd reach adulthood.

Let's look at something as simple as missing the bus after school. On this day, I decided to walk home instead. I needed the space to think over my week, to assess what I was going back home to, and to build in a new action plan. The main purpose was to come to some kind of calm before getting home. I was delaying the next likely attack.

I knew I'd have to climb through my bedroom window when I got home - so I didn't flag the lateness. If I was seen arriving late, I'd be beaten senseless. If I avoided being seen, I wouldn't be noticed until the next day.

If I didn't take the time to think, didn't plan ahead, or wasn't flexible enough to bounce - I learned my lessons harder. So, it meant I sometimes took a chance like this, and the risk was usually worth it for the insight I gained.

Everything was so topsy-turvy, I never really knew which way was up. It became vitally important to understand why people said what they said and did what they did, so I could try and protect myself from further harm.

Part of the legacy of my childhood suffering came from the more obvious physical, mental and emotional traumas inherent in a dangerous childhood environment. The biggest impacts, though, reached much greater depths and were far less apparent.

These early, disturbing experiences set me on a path to discover the secrets of how the world worked.

I believe it's important to learn through each moment in its fullest and to release the valuable lessons hidden within. In asking for insight, I am delivered opportunities to grow. So, I keep searching. So, I keep questioning. If that means I must break down inner walls in order to rebuild myself into a more magnificent version of me, then so be it.

Summing it all up, it's what my life really is for. Facing great difficulty has helped with developing a kind of super resilience that beats the odds. Most people I know don't explore the range of experience I have moved through and overcome. It takes everything you have. The grand prize though, is the phenomenal toolkit you walk away with; accumulated from every encounter that tested you to the extreme. The advantage of such experience and its true value, is only fully recognised in hindsight. The lesson must be learned for its magical mystery to be uncovered.

The true voice of the lesson lies in the reckoning.

I found my essential powers as a woman after years and years of misidentifying myself - choosing not to be fully me for the longest time. And there are lots of reasons for that. I have since come to a full appreciation of the 'gifts' trauma has presented to me, and the depth of personal growth that was necessary because of it.

The more resourceful you become, the easier it is for you to be able to resolve any situation that appears, regardless of how insurmountable the obstacle seems. I believe there is nothing we can't overcome, if we have the desire to do so. The problem is, on the most part, we don't necessarily want to see all the pieces of the puzzle that we want to solve. The magic is hiding in there, though. And the true essence of the woman comes out of appreciating it all. Both light and dark.

I began to realise my own innate ability from an early age. I remember a particular day, when I was five years old. It was a Day of Reckoning. I'd lived through so much. Processing life and death decisions, riding the sanity rollercoaster, driven to protect my siblings, and barely coping. Mentally exhausted, I had walked two kilometres to my favourite spot in the Blue Mountains bush and sat right next to a waterfall. Listening to the sound of the water, feeling the grass and rocks under me and being completely surrounded by the comfort of nature, brought about a surreal awareness ... kind of like a dream.

So, I sat in an almost meditative state, choosing to be at peace, allowing the reality of my life to drift further away from my thoughts.

And I had a vision.

I saw myself standing on top of a mountain with my arms open wide, people coming from everywhere to hear what I had to say. To listen to my message. To come and take a piece of gold. And to take a bit of the magic away with them too. I had a voice! For the first time, I had a voice! I could see it. I could feel it. I was breathing in the

air of that vision and knowing it to be true, even though I didn't know what it meant. My reality as a five-year-old child living beyond my years, seemed less relevant in that moment. I knew then that my life was about something so much greater than me. It was my true self speaking out. My true feminine self.

At the age of six, I recall an incident that happened during a School Fun Run. Not so 'fun' for me because I lost my way.

I remember noticing how beautiful the sky was. Seeing the puffy light clouds in the rich blue sky as I was running aimlessly along the side of the highway. There was a lady pushing a pram, types of cars I hadn't seen before, and heat shimmering on the footpath. I usually spent a lot of my time in a dream state like this - it was a great coping strategy. I daydreamed a lot. My internal world was rich with colour and warmth, a nice made-up version of what I imagined the world could be. When playing make-believe, I felt whole, I felt safe. So, I spent a lot of time there.

On this particular day, I only became aware as a car pulled up next to me. "I don't know where I am", I remember thinking. I felt lost and confused staring blankly at the strange man in the driver's seat. He said to me, "I know your parents and I can take you home". That day, I took a ride with a random stranger alongside the Great Western Highway.

That could have been my very last day.

Now, as an adult with my own children, I'm acutely aware of the possible consequences of accepting that ride. Thank goodness he was genuine and he did take me home.

I could run through 1000's of examples of moments in my life that challenged the odds, like this one. To share them all and all the learnings attached, would take us more time and space than we have here right now.

So, I'll share some magic instead.

Regardless of the prevailing circumstances ...

Dreaming is a great way to slow your heart rate and mind chatter, enabling rest and recovery.

Friendship with self is essential to ensure you have your own back and can keep yourself safe.

Being clear-headed is worthwhile when perceiving danger, to allow yourself the opportunity to assess and manage the situation.

Feedback is a beautiful way to balance your internal world against the external world, and to see where you want to draw the line.

Being the best version of yourself, requires that you put your oxygen mask on first. It's important to give deliberate attention to the quality of life you choose for yourself each day.

I believe the essence of an empowered woman is in her flow, in her intuition, in her love, and in her ability to live in her truth. And the extent to which these are played out, emphasises her femininity.

Women quite naturally think, feel and speak in flow - like a ribbon floating in the breeze. It's a beautifully expressive labyrinth of emotional content with anchor points for context, meaning and relationship associations. We are closer to the dream state when in our natural flow. The direct, linear and compartmentalised thinking we often see in the males we know, is magnificently contrasted, and just as essential to the outcomes we seek. Men are closer to the action state when naturally engaged.

Unfortunately, the socially acceptable myths which say that ...

1. Women are more emotional than men, and

2. Men don't understand feelings

... are terribly misguided and devalue the beautiful richness that is found in the genuine nature of both. Both men and women (however masculine or feminine they may be) feel deeply. Sometimes it's expressed through language or tone or action, or even inaction. We all do it differently. The gift is in understanding the beautiful depths and truest nature of every person with whom we connect.

The reality of appreciating all the people we connect with, is a learning adventure on its own.

When I chose to combine my personal life and my business life, my marriage partnership tested this truth.

It was a marriage that was probably more like a dictatorship than a partnership, if I describe it more accurately. Despite my profound childhood vision, I didn't yet have a voice. And regardless of the mental and emotional needs of our children, I had to work. And that was it. No discussion.

So, my son went to childcare while I worked in full-time employment.

One day (while pregnant with my second child) my eldest son opened up to me for the first time. He shared his painful feelings about childcare, begging me not to send him back. My children had always come first for me, and as soon as I realised the impact childcare was having on him, my decision was made.

Against my husband's ruling, I decided to trial 'working from home'. I left my career as a scientist to start my first business.

At the beginning it was a massive juggle. Regular midnight arguments, baby not sleeping, business commitments, customer commitments, emotional breakdowns, school runs, and the unnoticed further impacts on my eldest son ... who didn't often communicate his feelings.

These were very hard times, with two main lessons that shone through it all.

Awareness: Be aware that every player in your game of life has an inside voice, even if there is no sound to be heard. Ask, listen, play, talk, tune in. So much can be lost in the moments you are focusing somewhere else. Awareness covers all 360 degrees.

Resourcefulness: There are always ways to attend to more, without consuming more of you. The more you see, the more resources you can utilise. We are often so trapped within or emotionally consumed by a problem or challenge we are faced with, that we don't see the options we actually have available to resolve it. Step back, identify the resources at hand and systemise what you can to help with next time.

The best decision I made (in the light of family and business) was to ensure that 16 years ago, I work from home. All this time I've been available, present and tuned into my boys' life journey - so they have what they need to become their best selves. They are amazing human beings, each exploring their own unique pathway through life. I have the heart of my business, its purpose, vision and mission in my sight at all times too. It means that Personal Leadership Academy also has what it needs to do what it's here to do.

There's a beautiful balance and a natural flow that comes about when you're living your truth.

Look, I still believe 'it's a man's world' to some degree. Maybe it's just because the majority of leaders, upper managers and owners of business are men, across the globe. It's a simple statistical fact. Interestingly, men are engaging more with their families than ever before, choosing flexible options to be around their children and home.

In contrast, more and more women are part of the workforce these days... occupying increasing numbers of leadership and upper management positions. Slowly and surely, women are becoming more acknowledged and appreciated for the role they play in the material world. It's a changing world with so many shades of grey, and hopefully a happy balance point out there in the future.

I believe the special attributes that make a woman successful in business are those that shine when she's in her truest personal power. Her presence then encourages genuine magnetism and an extraordinary capacity to influence.

This is her magic.

What holds a woman back from success is the baggage she carries from her past conditioning, especially the persistent thought of being somehow 'less than'. Regardless of the circumstance and regardless of how well she has masked it, if this inner beast is fed, it will disempower her and render her helpless.

The beast, guaranteed, will challenge her at the time she needs to be most fearless - when she's preparing to take a leap of faith.

In 2011, I made the momentous decision to invest in a $10,000 training program. I risked my marriage and friendships and upended my world, following my intuition to change my life.

And it did.

For the first time since my vision as a five-year-old, I felt my voice awaken … Could I really make a difference? Since the idea of Personal Leadership Academy had already been evolving inside me for so long, I chose to start learning how to help people with the deep resounding wisdom I'd developed over the years.

I met a man in a laundromat once. He just came over to me and said, "I feel that you have some value in my life. Can you help me?"

My 'Yes' invited him to start talking about his son with schizophrenia … he was having a hard time supporting his son effectively, as a single parent. My intuition kicked in and I somehow just knew I could help him through the day-to-day with his adult son. It wasn't long before he realised he could lead his life differently to what the 'instructions on the box' said. He no longer felt he was in a hopeless situation.

During the time I was supporting the father, I also started a conversation with the son. Despite all the professional services that were a regular part his life, our conversation led him to realise that he could do things, think things, and plan things, which he never thought possible. An awareness of his personal value was emerging for the first time, and he no longer felt helpless.

My gifts were surfacing. It was a whole new world. This is my WHY.

What this experience taught me was that we are often too quick to judge a book by its cover. If you take the time to start reading, you'll often see something that is more extraordinary than you could have imagined. It's just a matter of being open to a new possibility and choosing to turn the page.

Through embracing the strength, courage and truth behind my own story, I found I could help people find their true personal power. I became the leader that empowers, inspires and steps up in the face of life's challenges.

We are all tapped into a fundamental truth … from the depths of our soul space. There's an immediate trust. Permission to open up, to explore the senses. It's like your unconscious mind is saying 'OK, YES! It's time to be me.'

This is the voice of your true self.

Intuitively, I know that navigating all aspects of personal leadership is really the key that opens this best version of ourselves.

Personal leadership is about having what you need internally to get back up after you've been knocked down, and standing up tall when it's important to face the music. It also involves just getting on with it when there's no puff left, when it feels like there is no hope, or when there's an impossible obstacle to move beyond. That tiny flicker of something in you that just drives you through the mud until you can see the light.

Learning how to listen to that little something inside you, is so important.

Everybody has the innate guidance system within them: sometimes tickling your interest, sometimes pushing and shoving at you, sometimes screaming crisis and demanding attention. Regardless, when answering 'YES' to any opportunity that appears, and taking that very first scary step … you are choosing YOUR journey, the road less travelled, and that makes all the difference.

Bringing forth the wisdom of my life's learning, I have designed a training mechanism for identifying and enhancing your amazing attributes and talents. Your true genius, when recognised, is your unique value to the world. Creating the key to your fulfilment has become my preoccupation.

Personal Leadership Mastery™ is my life's work.

It's amazing how much of my life experience has actually gone into the summary of the learning modules.

It has made my life worthwhile.

Each of the programs at Personal Leadership Academy cover FOUR deliberate cornerstones:

- DIRECTION ... Discover WHAT you are here to achieve.

- REFLECTION ... Determine WHY it's so important.

- CONNECTION ... Design HOW you will get there.

- INTEGRATION ... Consolidate, Align, Take a Step.

Natural progression through the training modules enables the gentle unfolding of deep-set conditioning - allowing the mind to embrace some things and let go of others, as a matter of choice. The outcome is always worthwhile, exceeding your expectations every time.

Personal Leadership Academy turns your personal experience of life into a path of no regrets, and the manifesto of your potential greatness. I dive deeper into the human psyche, with a very practical approach, to help you navigate your untapped potential. Purpose, integrity, honour and wisdom form the foundation of the training programs – ranging from Introduction through to Mastery level certification.

What's inside you is your unique genius, the true magnificence of who you are, awaiting your best decision yet.

The decision to say 'YES!'

No one has the right to say you can't be who you are. No one. Because you've got to live with you, your whole life. So, the only person you need to answer to, is you.

That doesn't mean the world is to be ignored or that you must be isolated from it in order to be your true self. It also doesn't mean that you have to join the many leaders that think being 'a shark' is the only way to face the world. What it does mean is that you can choose to chip away at the framework you've built around 'what should be' and build a stable and nurturing environment that fits with the 'true you'.

I've had many types of failures and successes in my lifetime. I've been twisted, shaped and moulded by yuckiness over and over again. And despite the years of hardship and learning, I have always been my own best friend. I know who I am. I trust myself. I've got my back. I choose to be me every time.

My inner purpose is the breath that I breathe every single day. And this lifelong dedication to personal leadership has definitely helped many people to live a more empowered and enriched life.

As one of my clients so beautifully described, "Before this, I felt like I was living day-to-day wearing a mask and hiding my true personality from the world. For so many years I tried an array of out-reach help (such as counsellors and self-help seminars) with no real permanent effect. Since my completion of the training, a lot of things have shifted for me. I am confident in saying that I am finally PRESENT in all aspects of my life. I feel free to express myself openly and honestly without reservations. My past is no longer affecting my present behaviour. I strongly feel and KNOW that this program has allowed me to finally 'BE ME'."

Personal leadership is the best gift you can give yourself.

Who are you choosing to be today?

Ruth Posterino
Personal Leadership Academy

M: 0415 190 787
E: ruth@personalleadershipacademy.com.au
W: www.personalleadershipacademy.com.au

The founder of Personal Leadership Academy and creator of the Personal Leadership Mastery™ program, Ruth Posterino is known globally as a Catalyst for Success. Ruth helps leaders to find their true essence and the root of their genius, for the purpose of creating the life they want.

As you can imagine, through years of formal education and professional experience as a coach, trainer and corporate leader, Ruth has a considerable background in human behaviour and in the many expressions of the human psyche. It didn't start there, though.

As a young child, Ruth's unimaginable beginnings brought about a personal tenacity that had her learning to thrive in a whole new way. Nearly 45 years of developing her own unique resilience, courageous insight, and personal approach to uncapping human potential, has enriched the valuable resource of experiential wisdom, that is now available to you.

From Ruth's professional experience, the main reasons why leaders seek her guidance is when they are repeatedly experiencing burnout, their true voice is silent or silenced, their value has been under-acknowledged or misunderstood, or their genius has yet to shine.

In her chapter, Ruth will unearth the art of Personal Leadership Mastery™ through sharing the journey she's taken to discover her own genius. The valuable tools you gain along the way will not only inspire you to consider your amazing potential, they will also awaken you to the deep calling of your own true self. Inside you is the true magnificence of who you are, awaiting your best decision yet.

The decision to say 'YES!'

OFFER:

Own your true genius through the wisdom of Personal Leadership Mastery™...

the only formula harnessing the manifesto of your potential greatness. Curious? Let's book a time to chat!

go.oncehub.com/LetsHaveAChat

Photography © Leonie Magnuson

Activity

1. Who do you give your power away to?
What boundary do you allow them to consistently cross?
Why do certain people somehow rank above yourself?
When do you feel most disempowered?
Where do you feel the disappointment in your body?
How would MASTERING PERSONAL POWER strengthen your assertiveness?

2. Who are you choosing to be today?
What do you lose when hiding your true self?
Why is it necessary to mask who you are?
When does this masking mostly occur?
Where is the line you will draw in the sand?
How would MASTERING YOURSELF ignite your spark?

3. Who do you know that lives in their true genius?
What is it about them that you so admire?
Why is that important to you?
When do you notice that same attribute showing up in yourself?
Where is that value hidden in you?
How would MASTERING YOUR GENIUS intensify your purpose?

4. Who is the internal voice you hear the loudest?
What compels you to listen to it?
Why is there ever a conflict?
When does your intuition kick in?
Where is your insight most significant?
How would MASTERING INTUITIVE INSIGHT deepen your perspective?

5. Who knocks you down when times are tough?
What specifically musters your courage to stand back up?
Why does it take so much energy and focus sometimes?
When would you like to be free of this burden?
Where does this situation keep showing up?
How would MASTERING RESILIENCE accelerate your achievements?

Helping you take control of
your financial future

> 'If you have ever taken a bullet to the heart, you'll know what I mean. I realised there is no point putting 'band-aids on bullet wounds' – GW

How did Genene Wilson become a talented Money Manager and Financial Planner?

She was born in the Swinging Sixties amid an emerging generation gap, anti-war protests, the movement toward greater equality for women, and the beginning of legal recognition of Aboriginal and Torres Strait Islander peoples. All these social changes made a unique impression on Genene, moulding her into the unique person she was to become.

"Home life for me was very sheltered, and I would say conservative. Dad was a hard-working man and mum was a tea-totalling homemaker. We travelled around Australia quite a lot as kids, especially after dad became ill and could not continue to work in his trade. We moved houses and changed schools quite a few times too, which lead me to feel that wherever you are is home - something that has stayed with me to this day. 'It's just geography ... It is a lack of lasting attachment to bricks and mortar', I thought."

Genene does not remember much conversation taking place at home. Children were to be 'seen and not heard'. Many women and girls of her age had parents who told their daughters not to worry about money or a career, because they would be sure to get married.

"Well, it is.

"I have a distinct memory of not wanting to accept that fate. I could not wait to get to school, which I started at just four-and-a-half years old. I had a voracious appetite for knowledge and learning. I always planned on going to university, even though as a child I knew that far fewer women than men did end up studying at university. My parents certainly did not plan on it, so as a young married mother with a child, I relocated my family from the New South Wales Central Coast to Western Sydney to attend university, at my own expense.

"Be careful what you wish for! It was hard work having a full-time corporate job, attending university part-time and running a household. I think that is when my Wonder Woman phase kicked in! Strength and self-reliance were my super-powers. My vulnerability was in trying to be all things to all people - to my family, my friends, at work, at university and in my industry - all of which drained me of my energy.

"If you have ever taken a bullet to the heart, you'll know what I mean. I realised there is no point putting 'band-aids on bullet wounds'. I felt that in the corporate world I was always waiting for the bullet to strike. I was uneasy and lived under a shroud of 'not being good enough'.

"I was bullied and stripped of my ego. And when you take one or many bullets over your lifetime, the surface may heal, but what lies beneath - not so much! That hurt and pain will sit there for years doing a lot of damage that you cannot see. It is messy. Unconsciously you will repeatedly attempt to deal with serious problems in an inadequate way, frustrating yourself, piling it on, building a mountain of resentment and making one misstep after another."

"I'd stuff down the feelings; especially the many times I was sexually harassed or bullied at work - I'd leave the job rather than call the offender to account for their actions. I would totally isolate those thoughts and feelings; you know, the ones that play on a loop in your head and make you miserable. You blame yourself 'Why you were so stupid …?', they steal your ego if the offender has not already done that job for you first!

"There was a problem - all that negative energy finds a way out at the most inconvenient time. My home life was a relatively happy one, a busy working family. But sometimes, I would shock and embarrass myself when I would lose my cool at the shop because my order was mucked up, or some little thing would trigger me. All that awfulness that was compartmentalised would spew out.

"The most challenging opposition I ever faced was from my parents. When I met my future husband, naturally, he met my parents. Looking back, I do not believe they immediately 'hated' him, but events that unfolded shortly afterwards caused them to reject him as a future life partner for me. We were not great communicators in our family. Mum never clearly articulated why she did not like him. My dad avoided him for weeks when he attempted to ask for 'my hand in marriage', as was the custom, and when he was eventually cornered dad was dismissive. More than 37 years on, we are still together. Only in the last few years has the unpleasant reality struck me that all the denial of my feelings has built quite a bit of resentment inside me and contributed to my poor health."

Ultimately, in late 2018 Genene's body failed her.

"I woke up on December 1st, 2018 in idyllic Hawaii, unable to move my head, neck and shoulders, suffering intense pain. Following spinal surgery in April 2019, I was recovering at home, attending therapy and happy that the surgery was successful. Unbeknownst to me a rather sinister, insidious health problem was yet to be diagnosed. By mid-2019 I was unable to walk with ease, lift my arms, drive the car and in significant pain again. I was confused because my early signs of recovery were so promising; it wasn't until I almost drowned at the local hydrotherapy pool that I laid out all the symptoms to my GP. Initially I was diagnosed with PMR an autoimmune disease (typically found in people over 70!!); symptoms of GTA followed. I felt like I was in a revolving door of doctors, medical specialists, drug treatments including chemotherapy and all the side effects that come with it, without a great deal of success. I'm currently questioning being a customer for life of 'Big-Pharma' and alternative treatments. The fight is real!

"The daily grind of putting on the black and white pinstripe suit (sic! armour) and working really hard in my corporate job, and my clients' wellbeing was all-consuming. At the end of the day, I felt apathetic, exhausted and overwhelmed. I swung back and forth between my passion for helping people and being in the exit lounge of corporate life. I was mentally tired and physically sick, with no energy to live my dream life. Eventually, the discontent and disconnection became a compromise my family and I were unwilling to make."

She felt as if there were two people inside her body. First, the corporate businesswoman; dedicated, shrewd, a people pleaser, devoid of any true feelings. Then there was the other woman; a homemaker, mother, friend, outwardly seeming to have it all and be in control. This is a place in which MANY women find themselves. The truth was, she was avoiding her true feelings, lacked self-care, and she was frustrated and resentful.

"My purpose became clear during those months of recovery. I did a lot of mindset work with my Executive Coach Evonne E. and became comfortable believing in my own worthiness. I realised that if that happened to me, a smart entrepreneur, it could happen to anyone.

"As I started to do the deeper work on myself, I recognised that other women wanted to rebuild their lives and happiness too, and to take control of their financial situation (particularly if they have been through a traumatic event). I understood that it is about finding a rebalance and using their feminine energy to unlock the new life of their dreams."

In 2018 she resigned from a large financial services corporation because she felt her values - and women's values in general - were unappreciated and out of alignment. She founded her own financial services practice, Finesse Financial Advisers, in August of that year.

Here is how she describes the situations in which many women today find themselves:

- Prince Charming may have shown up on his steed, but he has not hung around! Approximately 50% of first marriages in Australia end in divorce and about 75% of second marriages. Clearly not happily ever after!

- Many young girls are fed fairy tales, but it is not just fairy tales that lead you astray. Often women dream of winning the lottery or anticipate a big inheritance, so they put their worries aside. Instead, they should be setting goals, learning or honing their financial skills.

- Even successful relationships/marriages end in divorce or death. Each person in the relationship needs to be able to stand on their own feet. This holds doubly true for women, who are generally financially and economically disadvantaged compared to their male counterparts.

"When starting my own practice in 2018, I spent significant time considering mission, vision, goals, values and people strategy - including culture. It is essential to me that the practice aligns with my view of the world and that I work with people who embody these energetic qualities that are important to me. I want my clients to have a consistent experience that aligns with who they see me as. At its core, that blueprint remains largely unchanged, however, has evolved as we embrace 'win or lose; learn'.

"The biggest things I see holding women in business back are their mindset, fears and biases. Doing the internal work is so important to future success. Sometimes you have to just start the business and then as it - and you - change deal with whatever comes up.

"My passion is to improve outcomes for women, because every woman is worthy of a bright happy future. The business idea was reborn, with a focus on women who were going through some sort of traumatic life event (like separation or divorce, death of a partner or significant person in their life, having to step back due to ill health); women who would benefit from rebuilding, perhaps from the ground up. Another realisation was, that focusing in on the money without addressing what is going on across all areas of one's life, just did not work. People talk about holistic advice, but I wanted to deliver life-changing advice."

Grinding herself into the ground until her health failed was the turning point. Just three short months after launching her business, Genene knew she could not go on. Firstly, she had to deal with her immediate health issues, and then she needed to build a team of people around her to tackle all aspects of her life - to set her on a new enlightened path. Doing the work on the inside, being accountable to herself, and releasing herself from the negative emotions by acknowledging her feelings and behaviours made her realise her feminine power and helped her to understand that she is one woman not Wonder Woman.

Genene can now rationalise the setbacks, problems and challenges she has faced over the years. But as her executive coach, Evonne E pointed out in a session one day, many of the behaviours and feelings come down to how she identified culturally. She had always felt an affinity for the land, water and indigenous people, but didn't quite understand how she fit in as she lived in white Australia. To her, it felt like a shameful secret, a truth, not to be shared for fear of being found out and treated 'less than'. Eventually, she overcame that fear. There were other secrets too, including that her grandfather served in the war and suffered PTSD, a horrible affliction.

Today, she apologises unreservedly for those secrets and lies.

We asked Genene to define what it means to her to be a woman. What is the essence of femininity?

"To me, the essence of a person (whether woman, man or child) is at their core. That essence differs as we are all unique. I could say that a woman is nurturing, loving, caring and sharing. At the same time, she may be pure, graceful, beautiful, strong, resilient, self-reliant, purposeful and just. Women are like a beautiful elixir; an exotic blend of essential ingredients and extracts, curated over time. Women are not perfect, and neither am I! I do not want to man bash; I like being in the company of men. Are men different? I do not believe so; they can be as nurturing, loving, caring, strong, self-reliant and as purposeful as women, but they have a different blend. Don't we all!? It all depends on how we use our feminine and masculine energy.

"At the very heart of it (for me) is the difference between feeling and thinking. Feminine is represented by feeling, whereas thinking is aligned with masculine energy. I believe it is up to us all to curate the person we want to be. If you do not like something about yourself, set about changing it by doing the internal work. That being said, I do not think it's fair if you try to change the other person you're in a relationship with. They have to want to make changes for themselves. And you cannot care more for them than they do for themself!

"Women are resilient, and from my observation more willing to address whatever challenges they are facing. They are more willing to seek help, they are persistent and do the work that is necessary. I have been working in a male-dominated industry for decades and for a very long time felt like I was in a game of 'whack-a-mole!' Every time I stuck my head up to share my vision or intuition on a subject, I would be knocked back down. That can certainly hold anybody back, but I believe it is a more prevalent experience for women in corporate or public life. Joining relevant professional associations and taking on leadership roles, can assist in changing the 'authority' over time; so can raising your influence and being seen and heard. More women are emerging as courageous, no longer allowing the masculine to hold them in their shame and guilt."

Today, Genene is a women's finance specialist who recognises that many women she meets are not confident about money and investing. Often, they are being paid less and taking career breaks to raise their family and performing a lot of unpaid work. And through other life events - such as the death of a partner, separating and divorcing, redundancy, desire to escape the daily grind of corporate life and ill health - women fall substantially further behind financially than their male counterparts.

"Finesse Financial Advisers was born to help women take control of their money, improve their understanding of money matters, protect themselves and their families, build their investment portfolio and wealth, and plan a bright, happy future. Another important aspect is in 'product development' niching down as we built a picture of our ideal client. We don't want to work with everybody, we want to attract women who are receptive to our ideas, who are in flow (or want to be) and who also want to live for joy."

Genene has sound advice for her clients:

Having money systems is fundamental to financial discipline - set good foundations, pay attention, get control and stay in control by regularly reviewing. Each year take a look at your money and reflect on how things are going for you. Celebrate what's working and plan out your next steps.

- Know your numbers - look after yourself.

- Seek to understand investments - listen and learn!

- Control costs and choices.

- Set GREAT goals for yourself and (as boring as it may sound) set a budget, build in emergency money and future needs, review regularly and adjust accordingly.

- Ignore 'Rent money is dead money'. Own where you can afford and live where you want!

- Ignore 'Don't worry about money, Prince Charming is on his way'. It may never happen. Learn to stand on your own two feet financially.

- Plan out your finances and make informed decisions.

- Do not sign up for things you do not understand!!

- Do not sign forms you have not read and understood.

- Do not buy investments you do not understand - keep asking questions until you do or pass.

- Regardless of who asks you (a loved one, family friend, adviser) DO NOT SIGN blank forms or go guarantor for someone unless you fully understand the ramifications.

- Do sit down regularly with your significant other and discuss money and goals. Also you should meet with your financial adviser annually or when your circumstances change.

Genene has done a lot of inner work in the past few years, especially on her boundaries. Her non-negotiables to work with clients one-to-one are there to help women find and strongly commit to the process. She only works with women who have a growth mindset and who value accountability. She does not do any one-off transactional work because she wants to provide life-changing solutions. She requires once weekly communication in the initial four-to-six-week period to successfully develop each client's unique financial plan. If a client cannot commit to this, it is not the right fit.

If a woman is not ready to commit or is not in the right head space, she respectfully declines to work with them and recommends do-it-yourself options until the woman is mentally ready. Genene also has strong relationships with other consultants to refer to if a client's 'problem' is not in her area of genius but needs attention.

Finesse Advisers offer a range of programs, tools and options for women seeking to make changes in their personal financial situation or business, including:

- Finesse Your Money podcast

- Bright Happy Future Scorecard to self-assess areas of vulnerability (goals, mindset, money systems and wealth strategies)

- Financial Freedom in Heels - a learning platform, which includes a 'how to build your own DIY plan'

- Financial Planning - signature FUTURE program, one-to-one to create your personal financial plan

- Workshops, boot-camps and retreats

- Money Mentor - strategic advice and long-term ongoing guidance

- A day with Genene - let's do lunch and discuss your money and business.

Genene is someone who has been through the corporate 'wringer' and has emerged successfully out the other side - having learnt some hard lessons along the way. She found out that she cannot do it all. As is the case with many women, she took on as much as she could handle - work, family and more - until she suffered a health breakdown. It was a wake-up call for her to launch her own business, helping other women to manage their finances and their lives.

Genene is passionate about helping her clients realise their dreams. Too many people leave their financial future to chance. She sees her role as facilitator, educator, mentor and financial coach. She helps clients to achieve their financial goals by providing them with clear cut and professional advice, allowing them to take control of their financial future.

"Every woman is worthy of a bright, happy future"
she says.

Clearly, she has found hers.

GENENE WILSON
Finesse Advisers P/Ltd

M: 0403 026 800
E: genene@finesseadvisers.com
W: www.finesseyourmoney.world

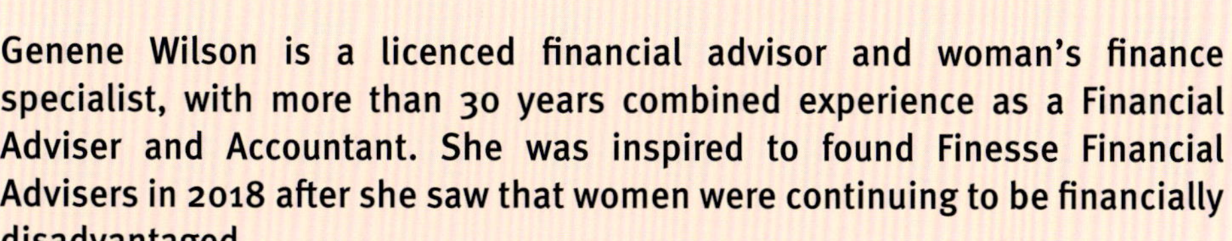

Genene Wilson is a licenced financial advisor and woman's finance specialist, with more than 30 years combined experience as a Financial Adviser and Accountant. She was inspired to found Finesse Financial Advisers in 2018 after she saw that women were continuing to be financially disadvantaged.

Genene believes that business has the power to change lives, "My job as a Planner is to look at clients' situation, goals, timeline, cashflow, investments, debt, their structure and risk factors. Often those things aren't understood but disjointed, like scattered jigsaw pieces with some missing. I orient the pieces providing the full picture". Getting control of 'the money' signals security for many women and is the springboard from which to rebuild and plan for a bright, happy future.

Becoming ill herself just three short months after launching the Finesse business caused a rethink. Suffering through challenging illnesses profoundly changed her view, forcing her to realise her life was completely out of balance. She'd been unconsciously making misstep after misstep, dealing with big problems in a small way. And, playing small!

Genene had been avoiding every signal her body sent bringing her to an intersection. She could continue building a mountain of resentment and laundry list of perceived failures or STOP. She chose to stop, deal with her immediate health issues, do the internal work taking time to recover. Then, rebuilding from the ground up.

During her time of healing and self-discovery Genene realised her passion was to improve outcomes for women. Saying "It's personally rewarding to help women realise their goals and dreams, especially if they have to rebuild financially after a traumatic life event".

Genene enjoys life with her husband Mick. She focuses on wellness and being chemical-free in her Western Sydney home. Genene enjoys time with family and friends, and hosts a book club each month, which is affectionately called the Tsundoku Social Club. She loves nothing more than discussing movies on a Friday evening with friends virtually in the Phyl-em Club.

LEGAL STUFF: Genene Wilson is an Authorised Representative of FYG Planners Pty Ltd. Finesse Financial Advisers is a Corporate Authorised Representative of FYG Planners Pty Ltd.

OFFER:

Curious about how we can help you?

Let's start with a 20-minute Discovery Call.

Book today at www.finesseadvisers.com/book-now/

Valued at $165.

Photography © Melinda Hird Photography & Video
Website: www.melindahirdphotography.com.au

Activity

1. Do you have limiting beliefs stemming from childhood that affect your money mindset? Delve into your views and seek to understand why you feel that way. Slow down and examine the inaccurate conclusions you drew as a kid, and how would you feel if you could clear away those unhealthy money habits.

2. Do you have a secret shame about money? Consider where you feel out of control, disorganised, in a mess. What doesn't feel good for you; is it budgeting, too much debt, paying your bills late or spending too much. Plan out your next steps to regain control and feel into what life will be like without money worries.

3. Do you have a plan covering all areas of your life – health, energy, fun, family & relationships, money & freedom, learning, growth & giving? The foundations of any grand plan involve articulating what's important and what your goals are. It is essential you find the right balance to unlocking the life of your dreams.

4. Are you using your money wisely & investing wisely with an expectation of a return? Invest in yourself, your business and assets - to grow your wealth and set yourself up for the future.

____

____

____

____

____

If you answered "Yes" to question 1 & 2 and "No" to 3 & 4, my story or activities piqued your interest, complete the full Bright Happy Future Scorecard. Available at https://future.scoreapp.com/ to assess your vulnerabilities, obtain your free report, including tips and clear action steps.

LINDA DEL AMOR

Founder and Director, Divine Feminine Reset Program
and Bodyscents Natural Skincare

Igniting a devine
feminine reset

> *'Attached like cords of energy within my body,*
> *I recognised all the waves of emotions that*
> *I had been denying'* – LD

I never thought it would be me.

I had fallen to my knees, shaking from the core, not being able to control the emotion as the tears rolled down. The feeling was out of control. Here I was with my children at the Perth Royal Show - where my Dad used to take me as a child - on what was usually a fun day out for my family.

A mix of memories of love and loss came to me as waves of emotion that I couldn't seem to process, and it led to feelings of anxiety. Memories of fun family days with my children's father all meshed together overlapping my own childhood memories. Yet here I was now, just myself and my children, and it all began to sink in. Had I repeated the pattern?

I was falling apart, unravelling and it wasn't fun. My hands began to shake. I heard the rides whirling around me and could smell the familiar scent of popcorn and warm doughnuts. These were once my favourite things, yet for some reason, now they evoked a lifetime of memories that felt sad and tragic.

Attached like cords of energy within my body, I recognised all the waves of emotions that I had been denying. The pain of abandonment, the fear of the men in my life, helplessness, grief. They had been unknowingly suppressed under the facade of 'I'm doing great, thanks'.

I had previously moved through many obstacles in my life and made it look effortless. 'You're amazing. How do you do it all?' I would get asked. Now I couldn't even manage to hold my own weight upright. I tried to rush out of there and find a place to hide.

I realised later it was a panic attack.

I had been brave enough to leave a toxic marriage but now I had no idea who I was on my own. Flying solo for the first time in 20 years (with four children and self-employed) this was a leap of faith, and I had to admit I was scared (this 'episode' clearly highlighted that and much more).

I needed to get to the root cause of my personal crisis and heal my deeper wounds. So, I became my own healer. That became my mission, while going through the motions of all that comes during times of family break up. I focused on my family and my skincare business - I became my only VIP healing client.

My subconscious mind had been running on outdated programming, so it was triggering old fears and adrenal overload of fight/flight responses, which had been there since birth. I like to think of this moment as the day my system got a wakeup call to reset.

There on my knees my ego was telling me 'Get up, don't let your girls see you so weak'. I felt the sting of shame and panic overcome me - it was like there was a battle going on inside me. I made a deal with God to heal from the past and become the best version of myself, for my children. 'Don't let my little girl see me like this. Please help me up. I promise to do whatever I need to do. I give in … I surrender.' I overcame my ego and I asked for help. My little girl was only four then and she called me her 'Queen'. I didn't feel like one then. I felt undeserving.

Many people are ashamed of feeling anxiety and it is particularly frightening when this manifests itself as a panic attack. This experience was foreign to me even though I'd seen many clients in the past with anxiety. I realised that my own healing journey would have to go deep - to up-root the perceived emotional blockages within my body and mind. Part of my journey from that moment to where I am now is my life's work, not just for myself but for the hundreds of women that have experienced my programs and healing sessions since then.

Falling to your knees can be the start of a beautiful journey, which allows you to rise more empowered than ever before. It could all be part of a divine plan to get us to simply be vulnerable enough to surrender. Now I understand, that at the moment your knees are about to hit the floor a beautiful grace takes over. A softening into the grace of the divine feminine that is giving herself over in an act of brave vulnerability. It takes faith to know you will be supported. Not giving in but giving it up to the universe - knowing it will all work out in the end. There is a time to fight and a time to surrender. In your divine feminine flow, you will intuitively know what is right for you in the moment.

It takes courage to lean into the shadows and be fearless in pursuit of your own purpose and happiness.

Each story of your past has a cord of attachment to your emotional body. We tend to assign a great deal of meaning to events and develop 'false beliefs' around them. Once released it can ultimately lead to a great deal of freedom and peace. . Unravelling the invisible cords and the links to your subconscious mind are powerful healing processes that I now guide people to do in my Quantum Healing Divine Reset sessions. These sessions allow you to come back to a place of neutrality and peace. They also heighten your own super conscious abilities without all the distractions of your past thoughts, feelings and behaviours. Once done my clients receive upgrades to their energy field and drop into a state of higher alignment (with what they desire and ultimately attract).

My work as a coach and a healer have helped me to live my life in alignment with the values of a divine feminine in her power, as a role model to my children and a mentor to my clients.

I come from a long line of strong women. The women on both sides of the family were interested in politics and world events, each was educated and strong. They were all fiercely independent in their own way. They all seemed to have absent hard-working husbands, unfortunately many of them abusive in different ways. That combined with the social norms of the day did not allow them the opportunity to really be in their own personal power or reach the potential that is possible for us as women today. I wonder what my ancestors would think of my Divine Feminine Reset Program now. They could never have imagined then that such programs existed and could help develop their intuition and Divine Feminine Power. We have come a long way as women since then and we still have a long way to go.

They say 'Hurt people hurt people' and that seemed to be the case with both my parents. They were a volatile separated couple and, while it was the highlight of my week when dad would come to visit, it wasn't regular and often led to incidents where I would need to run or hide. Despite the conflict with my mother and his very wounded past, he was an incredibly infectious good-looking man, generally kind with a big laugh and great charisma that was unforgettable. He encouraged deeper enquiry and intuition and would ask me "What do you think Lindy? Tell me from your gut, then I know it's the truth". I love that he trusted my intuitive guidance so strongly and gave it significance.

My mum was a driven, determined woman with a strong will to overcome her circumstances, and set an example to us by her achievements. She worked extremely hard, raising three children solo including my brother who has a disability. She did this while studying for a university degree part time and running a social group on weekends for people with disabilities. I would spend my Saturdays, after ballet and drama classes, working as a volunteer at these groups - under duress I might add. I actually enjoyed it, though, and learnt a lot from the experience.

My mother appeared to have strong feminist values of the day. Despite this, she chose men who challenged her in every way, especially with violence. That is something that both haunted me and baffled me as it seemed at odds to what I believe feminine power is. I loathed to see her as a victim. I think early feminists perhaps focused on challenging men rather than to try to understand and nurture them. Mum raised me to be extremely independent from a young age. So much so that I have had to consciously work on the fact that it is okay to ask for help. It took me a long time to understand the quote 'ask and you shall receive'. It's true, magic can happen when you ask to receive and place a great intention behind it.

My mother remained a complicated woman and we spent a great deal of time misunderstanding each other. Despite this, I believe we always get what we need and although I didn't have the bond that I most desired with her, I received a lot from her and in turn put a great emphasis on mothering my own children.

As a result I learnt; that we must overcome our own shadow selves and the past, so we have the ability to be vulnerable to love; to soften and receive love that is aligned to our values; to accept all the joy and abundance that is ours to have; that we must trust ourselves and let go of all need to control others.

Our Nanna, Ursula was an integral part of our world. She was the love and light in my life, and I often told her she would be my best friend if we had been from the same generation. She was the most glamourous, charismatic old lady I knew. She made life look graceful. Most knew her as affectionate, warm and generous, as having kindness and a cracking wit. As she died, I saw her soul leave before her heart stopped and as it did, a piece of my heart went with her. She remains one of my greatest mentors.

Growing up, I was mostly left to my own devices. So, I left home, very young, to explore and take on the new adventures of travel. I met my then guru (at aged 11) who taught me self-expression, meditation and visualisation, (which I continue now) to search out many alternative paths of inquiry and study.

I started my entrepreneurial career hiring space at a local herbal shop for massage, spiritual healing and aromatherapy blending for all kinds of ailments. As customers began asking for my creams, my 'accidental' start in business began to take shape. My business later won awards – my favourite was 'The Spirit of Australia' – as my skincare brand became global with online sales and distribution into SouthEast Asia. Fast forward a few years and many more diplomas, and I became the owner of my own clinic (for pain and stress management), while selling my skincare products commercially. As I continued to develop my gifts in healing and intuitive guidance, I also experienced massive personal growth. This led to my business growing in different directions as I earned many new certificates and the ability to help women (anywhere in the world) with my experience and skills that now include NLP Master Life Coaching and Hypnosis.

After my second marriage ended I sold what had been my 'dream home' (by way of a small miracle as it was not for sale). I asked god for a buyer for a quick exit, without expectation since most logical thoughts would be how could I sell a house secretly that was not for sale? ... Yet as if by direct answer to my calling.. three days later a buyer called, then emailed and showed up at the house. They made me an offer I couldn't refuse in a private sale. In many ways things were working out even though it still felt like I was losing 'the dream'. Things have to be torn down sometimes so they can be rebuilt anew.

I bought my own home right away. It felt like a huge achievement to have only my name on the title. It was mine to share with my family – a home where we were safe. My eldest daughter said she was 'proud of me' and that meant everything.

I always knew how to manifest things in my life. It came naturally to me to think about something, and it would happen. I didn't know how - I just did it. If I wanted to travel somewhere, buy my dream home, or meet someone, it happened. It took me until now to break down the process enough to be able to teach it.

I choose to be here, so I can self-actualise in my full potential and power, while showing others to do the same. The time has never been more right to help guide others back to their bliss.

A woman in her divine power has the ability to tap into the unseen and speak for the unheard. A woman in her divine power has the ability to create life for others and herself giving life to her dreams in a way that is magical and vibrates with a resonance to a higher good. She can communicate what she wants clearly and is not pushy, needy or demanding. She has a knowing that is quiet and authentic. A divine woman in her power has a grace that others notice and feel touched by. It's a compassion and love for all beings. She is the mother, and she is the goddess, and she is the lover. She is effortlessly, authentically herself - and opportunity is easily attracted to that because her energy bands in her sphere are clearly able to articulate the right point of attraction.

Have you noticed when you feel particularly 'in flow' you only have to think about someone or something and it comes into your field? This is how energy and frequency match and attract each other. There's no limit to what you can ask for. There's an abundance of everything we desire out there. When you are in your divine power you can enter a room and just the right people come to you. You know the parking spot is always there. You can attract the highest potential partner for yourself without making lists of impossible demands - instead you are attracted by the power of the frequency that you both understand. Life becomes more effortless.

Prosperity is available when you are fully expressed in your own gifts. Your energy speaks way before you open your mouth. Even when we are not aware of it, we are picking up on those cues long before we even look into someone's eyes and listen to their words.

What I teach in my Divine Feminine Reset Program is how to master the state of your energetic blueprint or biosphere.

My Divine Feminine Reset Program focuses on communication, creativity and intuition - the most important aspects of our divine feminine. We need to communicate from the heart deeply and authentically in order to be fully felt, seen and appreciated, and to allow others to connect to us in a heart-conscious way. This is the softening. We must surrender our ego and pride in order to soften our spirit and tame the wildness of our shadows and our pain.

The Divine Feminine forgives easily and effortlessly. She manifests from a place of alignment in the knowing of the great spirit, 'Oneness'. Taking radical responsibility for our wounding and healing is crucial to bring transformation. I once chose idolising and controlling narcissistic relationships that didn't allow for truth and vulnerability, and relied more on looking good from the outside in. Completely at odds with my values though attuned to the pain frequency I was still holding in my sphere and emotional body.

It was only in the last few years that I really trusted myself to choose a partner from my heart and higher self, based on values and energetic attraction. I let my higher self guide me to an ancient connection with divine knowledge, and to explore a deeper love with myself and others. It invokes the kind of deep pleasure of discovery that awakens your senses fully.

The gift of receiving is the gift of the divine feminine.

You are and always have been divine. You were created in divine union regardless of how your creation came about… there was a plan to bring you here. Now what will you do with that? What purpose will you live for as a self-actualised woman? Such a worthy pursuit is finding the woman of your own dreams, your inner Queen. The greatest investments I have ever made are in my own growth and the mentors that helped guide me to find her, my inner Queen. She is always in a state of co-creation with others and with the universe, she is all of me. Knowing this, puts me in a state of flow and far away from where this story began. Contentment and happiness will be yours too when you take aligned action to your thoughts and desires and then simply receive.

I'm on a mission to bring women into alignment to their truth and discover their voice, their gifts and their full potential. Experience deep loving connection to themselves, God and others. Oneness is possible for all of us if we are ready to accept the golden truth of awakening to our power.

As a mother of three beautiful daughters and one son, I am very conscious of the legacy I leave in the world for them. My children have been by far my greatest teachers and inspiration. Each new generation is a chance to improve upon the last. In healing ourselves we heal generations after us. That is why I choose to work with women because we are the creators of life and so much more. We are the winds in the wings of our beloved masculine partners. Women are going into business in much larger numbers and I am here to mentor and support them to create their impact on the world.

Life may not have been a fairy tale, but you get to be the Queen. You are responsible for the part you play in your story and how it ends.

As Marianne Williamson said "Our deepest fear is not that we are inadequate. Our deepest fear is that we are powerful beyond measure. It is our light, not our darkness, that frightens us most. We ask ourselves, who am I to be brilliant, gorgeous, talented, and fabulous? Actually, who are you not to be?"

I believe that we haven't even come close to our full human potential. You have Divine Feminine Power. You've had it all along.

It's time to ignite it.

LINDA DEL AMOR

Divine Reset

M: 0481 322 265
E: linda@divineresetnow.com
W: www.divineresetnow.com

Linda helps women engage their purpose and reach their full potential in life. She particularly loves to work with change makers and entrepreneurs, to help them attract and magnetise more love and abundance in their lives.

Linda has been a loving mother, therapist and business owner for the past 25 years. She is a dedicated coach and mentor to many, and passionate about getting results that are immediate, measurable and lasting.

Linda delivers her coaching sessions and DIVINE RESET quantum healing sessions to almost anyone and anywhere in the world (with the help of technology). These sessions unravel cords of attachment to the past and remove negative emotional patterns of behaviour in the body, mind and bio-sphere (energetic blueprint) of the client. While the client is under hypnosis she can more readily remove limitations in the subconscious mind and use NLP and somatic work with soul journey work in the same session for maximum results.

'Divine Feminine Reset Program' is an online experience that develops a woman's super conscious power for a more connected and fulfilled life. It assists women to engage all nine petals of power of the female psyche.

Linda founded her own international award winning natural personal care brand 'Bodyscents Natural Skincare' back in the 1990s and is still the head alchemist and CEO behind the company. Over the years it's estimated Linda has helped thousands of people move from pain to freedom and flow. Her passion is to lead people to their 'bliss'.

Linda is an experienced international group transformational retreat facilitator. She is a warm and engaging public speaker who inspires others around feminine empowerment that is creative, connected and magnetising.

Linda's qualifications include: Diplomas in - Clinical Aromatherapy and Health Science, Swedish Massage, Bowen Therapy. Certificates in: Emmett Technique, Aura Soma, Various Healing Studies. Master of Hypnotherapy, Life Coaching, NLP and Past Life Regression techniques.

OFFER:

Would you like to learn more about Divine Feminine Power and how to ignite YOUR own divine reset - for more peace, power, passion and prosperity?

Please go to Linda's website www.divineresetnow.com and download the free ebook Divine Feminine Reset. You can also receive a free meditation and 'Attraction Magnet' masterclass from Linda – which guides you to becoming an attraction magnet for love and abundance. This will help you to become open to receiving, so you can attract the right people, opportunities and money into your life with more ease, flow and grace.

Trust that you are in the right place and time to receive it now.

Go to: www.divineresetnow.com

Photography © Steve Green

Activity

1. If I had a magic wand to give you one awesome outcome for your life right now, what would that outcome be?

____

____

____

____

2. What are the one or two limiting beliefs that you identify as being in your way?

____

____

____

____

3. What actions can you take to remove these limiting beliefs in your life?

____

____

____

____

4. What values do you think you need to adopt in the area you identified above – values that will bring your desired outcome closer to your reality?

____

____

____

____

A healing journey to find wellness purpose and abundance.

> *'I wasn't a rebellious child but was always determined and strong-willed.'* – MM

Hey beautiful. My name is Min Melgar.

I was born in 1974, the eldest of two children and I grew up in the suburbs of Western Sydney, living there until I was 19.

I was a bright, straight 'A' student throughout my school years. I was very aware that my parents had high expectations of me, especially my father who is extremely intelligent, with a mathematical mind. I gravitated towards my dad and became known as 'Daddy's girl' by my mother and was often compared to him in terms of looks and ability. My brother, being the youngest, seemed to gravitate more towards my mother.

I wasn't a rebellious child but was always determined and strong-willed.

By the end of my school years, I had discovered my love for the Arts and creativity. I had always done well academically, but I shone in subjects like art drawing and music. Upon finishing my HSC, when I told my Dad that my dream job was to work as an Animator for Walt Disney and that I was looking into becoming a Graphic Designer, he was mortified. I remember him saying that I would never make any money in the Arts, and that I would have to be 'outstanding' in this area to get anywhere. His advice was to become an Accountant, Lawyer or professional, as I had the skill and grades to make it and be successful. I began to second guess myself and thought that maybe my idea of becoming a graphic designer wasn't so good after all. I had also been bullied for most of my younger years and had major self-esteem issues stemming from my weight, appearance and the constant negative self-talk that ran through my head. I decided to abandon my dream of becoming a graphic designer and studied accounting instead.

Looking back, I realise that this decision was largely about my need to please my father and to not 'disobey' his wishes. He was always in my corner, supporting me and loving me and only wanted the best for me.

I only started to discover my essential power as a woman when I began

running my own business back in 1999. I was 25 years old, a newly licensed female conveyancer, working in a predominantly male legal industry. Being a young, ambitious woman with authority was a difficult role, as women were generally employed as legal secretaries or paralegals. There were few female solicitors and conveyancers at the time, and the ones that were qualified were either belittled, disrespected, or talked about by all the other boys as 'ball breakers'. I remember several instances throughout my career where I took a stand on behalf of my business or my client (against a fellow Solicitor or Lawyer who had presented incorrect information) and was told many times to 'go back to being a paralegal'.

I started to feel that the only way to be shown respect by my peers was to conform to their ideals. The choice was to be feminine but not too much, or fear being ridiculed and the subject of their taunts or, be forceful and more masculine like they were, to gain their trust and respect. The incredible impact of these early years of my career in the legal industry would become shockingly apparent later in my life, when I went through divorce, separation, and almost losing my family and my health.

There were three major catalysts that lead me to realise my own innate ability and connection to my best feminine self. The first was my divorce. The second was my separation from my second husband, and the third was my health crisis.

Each catalyst brought me closer to my authentic self as a woman.

The Divorce

I married my high school boyfriend after eight years of being together. I was seventeen when we met during our last year of high school. I hadn't travelled Australia or the world, or even had a full-time job of my own. We married at 25 and almost three years in, our family and friends started asking when they could expect children? As much as I wanted children ONE DAY, I felt like I hadn't even begun to experience the world and all it had to offer. I started asking myself why I didn't feel ready to have children. I began finally listening to my inner voice, and the words that I was hearing made me feel selfish and ungrateful. I realised I had made a HUGE mistake. The wedding day 'jitters' that I had many months before we got married were being validated almost three years later. Who was I as a woman and a human being? I immediately had a sense of fear and dread. I realised that I had gone through with the wedding because it was what was expected of me. I was a 'good girl' and always did the right thing. I had also struggled fiercely with my parents and my own beliefs around being 'divorced'. My mother and father had been married for 32 years at this point. My mother's parents were married for over 50 years, as too were my dad's parents.

But the need to end this relationship out of the fear of losing myself was too strong. I ended it with my husband and faced the wrath of family and friends. The backlash was even stronger than I had anticipated. My father was furious with me. He didn't understand my reasons and his own beliefs were blocking him from being able to be supportive. My ex's brother also strongly voiced his opinions on the type of person and woman he now believed me to be.

I felt ashamed, guilty and alone. The low frequency emotions were almost too much for my soul to bear. I never wanted to hurt anyone. My mother completely trusted and supported my decision, as did close personal friends. They knew I had made this decision from my heart, and that it wasn't made overnight.

Separation

The separation from my second husband lasted seven months.

I truly believed I had found my soulmate when I met him. After the grueling first experience of heartache and divorce, I didn't expect to find 'the one' that could make my heart sing the way he did. I knew our relationship had some problems that needed attention, but I didn't realise how deep the complications ran.

After our son was born, I had dropped into my 'masculine action side' of running a business from home while working hard to ensure that I was helping provide for our beautiful little family.

I came from a hard-working, business-owner background, and believed that I didn't have to rely on my husband to be the only breadwinner in the family. I threw myself into making the business work. What I didn't do, was consider that taking this time away from my husband and the two of us as a couple, would detrimentally affect our relationship.

I found out that my husband had been unfaithful - and it rocked me to my very core.

It made me question my every thought, every ability and judgment. I felt extremely depressed, completely unhappy with myself, and I became physically and mentally ill. I lost all faith in my ability to trust anyone and became emotionally disconnected from my heart and mind, and even my family. It took me having thoughts of wanting to end my own life, to begin restoring my faith in myself and others again. Our son was the lifeline to overcoming my grief and sadness. I wanted nothing short of an amazing life for him and knowing that he too was sent to earth for a purpose, I began engaging with life again. I started taking care of myself more, exercising and trying new things like boxing and pole dancing, things I never thought I would EVER experience. I began cherishing all the moments my son and I had together. I started to use holistic and metaphysical therapies to work through my grief, self-sabotage and forgiveness. My son and I worked with a Kinesiologist (separately and together) to begin mending the pieces of our broken hearts. I began to heal my life. I stopped being a victim and consistently apologising. I began to fully step into the woman I was proud to be - living authentically and unapologetically.

Health Crisis

My health crisis came to a head on March 3rd, 2015.

I had been a yo-yo dieter all my life. Always on the new fad, low carb, low fat, high fibre, ketosis, Sureslim, weight watchers, Gloria Marshall, Jenny Craig, the cabbage diet, shakes, liquid diet. I had tried every diet that was published in a magazine. I had started putting on weight around age nine or ten after being extremely ill, and over the years I had become bigger and bigger.

As a teenager, all my friends had the most gorgeous boyfriends. I was the 'big girl' and was extremely self-conscious about my weight. I had heard the boys talking about their girlfriends with love and admiration, comparing each one on a scale of one-to-ten in terms of who was the prettiest. When it came to their rating of me, I was the big girl with the beautiful eyes and lovely heart but didn't have the body to match. I began drowning my emotions in food. I ate when I was stressed, I ate when I was happy or sad. Prior to my separation I had stopped looking after myself and the weight had started to creep back on. Add separation, a move away from family, another baby who was ill during her first year, two sleepless years following her birth, AND a full-time job in the mix - looking after myself wasn't a high priority.

I crashed and burned badly. I was in bed full-time for three months, and it took a further two years to bring my body back to a state of equilibrium.

I had stage four Adrenal Fatigue, Hashimoto's Thyroiditis, Fibromyalgia, Leaky Gut, Pyrrole Disorder, a host of vitamin and mineral deficiencies and little self-worth or vitality for life left. I had no choice but to nourish and nurture my physical, emotional, and spiritual bodies back to life. I was broken in every sense of the word. The masculine 'doer' in me didn't know anything about alignment and balance of these parts of myself. The doer kept doing. She never ever STOPPED. If I wasn't working, I was looking after someone else's physical or emotional needs, constantly pouring from an empty cup.

The Journey Back

The journey back led me through the complete destruction and death of who I thought I was, back to life and my true, feminine, powerful self. It wasn't easy. There were many steps backwards or sideways, without many forwards. I persevered and started to believe that my life here on earth was no accident, and that my purpose was to inspire and educate other like-minded women, so that they too could live a life of alignment, wellness, purpose and abundance. They too, could also find the way back to a deep connection to themselves.

I believe the essence of being a woman is connection to your true authentic self. There is a well-known yogic quote from The Bhagavad Gita that says, 'Yoga is the journey of the self, through the self, to the self'. For much of my life I felt disconnected from myself and my purpose. I felt that I knew what I wanted from an early age, but as I grew and became influenced by others (while going through my own experiences) I began trusting myself less - allowing the inner critic to take over. Experiencing trauma, grief, loss, love, joy and being able to truly accept and appreciate each as a lesson or life experience, has brought me closer to myself and also closer to the divine. I do not consider myself to be a religious person, however, now I have a 'knowing' - a deep sense of connection and truth that we are spiritual beings having a human experience.

Femininity is being able to express love and joy through yourself and your business, without feeling weak. Being vulnerable is a strength not a weakness, because in our vulnerability lies truth and wisdom. Femininity is showing compassion when needed and staying true to your inner knowing and conviction, surrendering to our creativity and radiance, and bringing these strengths into the masculine business world, creating ease and flow. Typically, most men come from a place of the wounded masculine, using dominance and aggression as a position of power and authority. Balancing the natural characteristics of both the feminine and masculine is the way forward.

Personally, I have found combining my business and personal lives, whilst juggling a career or business and children, to be challenging. I am an ambitious, driven woman and adjusting to a new normal whilst raising babies was difficult. I went back to my career only three months after our first child, Keanu was born. I had hardly recovered from the trauma of childbirth and the physical and emotional changes in my body. We were blessed that our boy was sleeping through the night from around eight weeks old. However, now looking back, I wish I had the insight and wisdom to have also tuned into MY body, allowing myself to re-energise, nourish, and nurture my own health needs. I know now that if I had, I would've been a less stressed, more balanced woman and mother. I was extremely lucky that I had the support of my husband and family during our son's early years, as my mother looked after our son allowing me to go back to work and advance further in my career.

The second birth was a little harder. I was 39, almost eight years older than when our first was born. We were also living away from close family and friends. I couldn't go back to my existing job, because I didn't want to go back to work full time. I had learnt from past mistakes and wanted to be able to have a more balanced home and family life. I also wanted to enjoy my time more with Charlize (as the time spent with Keanu had passed so quickly). I felt a sense of having a second chance to experience the amazement of childbirth and those early months. We had also lost a baby, two years prior to Charlize's birth, and this loss only made our connection with our beautiful girl even stronger.

But then our plans were thwarted. My husband was made redundant from his full-time, high-paying job the week we brought our baby home from hospital. As my husband had only had this job for a short period of time, there was no big payout or security net to fall into. The next six months were tough, playing catch up with my husband trying to secure another full-time job. He was able too, but not without accepting a massive reduction in salary. I decided to begin a new conveyancing business from home, to help our family get ahead and to reduce the weight that was falling heavily on my husband's shoulders.

Our daughter wasn't a healthy baby and she seemed to pick up ear infection after ear infection. She wasn't a good sleeper, and we were all feeling the effects of lack of rest. I know that financial restrictions, as well as my own belief systems, have contributed to the self-imposed struggles around balancing business and home life. We have overcome them by learning from our past mistakes. Time is precious and it slips by too quickly. My husband has stepped up his involvement in our home life and is now aware that if we are both working on our purpose and career, then we both need space to create them. He contributes so much more to our family on a personal level by spending time with the kids, cooking dinner and helping with housework.

Business is only one part of our lives, and if we place absolutely all our attention on this one area, there is guaranteed suffering and sacrifice in some, if not all, of the other areas. Our past had given us the gift of hindsight, which was to cultivate and create balance in all areas of life.

A woman that is confident in herself, connected and unapologetic in her conviction, with a purpose, a woman who comes from a place of love and alignment, is a powerful woman. A woman is naturally receptive and intuitive, and if aligned, comes from a place of unconditional love, ease and flow. These traits applied to our business can create a truly abundant, purpose-filled business and life. This type of business has the ability to change many, many other lives. Some women see these attributes as weaknesses and shy away from the business world, feeling that they may not 'make it' or be 'tough enough' to navigate their way through. Each one of these women has a powerful story to share, and without them owning their place and purpose, many others would not feel or experience the benefits of their wisdom and gifts. Our fears and our ego can be extremely powerful in our undoing. If we allow our inner critic to control our lives, we are held back from owning all of our successes. Society and past conditioning tell us that men are the rulers of the business world, and that women are meant to stay home, and make babies and a home. Past successful women like Oprah Winfrey have shown us that whoever you are, you have the ability to make a difference in the world.

"Don't worry about being successful but work towards being significant, and the success will naturally follow" – Oprah.

Most men are driven by success. 'Success = Money'. Most women are driven by purpose or significance, and how they can make a difference in the world. This version of success contributes to the whole of society on such a grand scale. It is unselfish, it is pure grace and innate intelligence. It speaks to the hearts and souls of others because as each woman rises up, so does her frequency and vibration. Her energy effects everyone around her, and when this energy is expansive, it has the power to raise the collective consciousness of the world.

Essentially Well

I began my business, Essentially Well, just over two years ago. It has morphed into a business of lifting women out of exhaustion and stress, and into wellness, purpose and abundance. My inner purpose of supporting women to holistically revise and rebuild their health, well-being and spirit has come from my own lived experience through debilitating chronic illness and fatigue. I know there are so many women out there like me. We have experienced the same journey, just on a different timeline. We have felt the depths of spiritual by-passing, becoming detached and emotionally numb from painful, unbearable experiences. We sat in periods of denial to our shadow sides, living out life with a false sense of security and happiness, convincing ourselves that we are fulfilled. Until very recently I didn't know that spiritual bypassing was a thing, or what it even meant. I understand this now to mean that it is an avoidance of unresolved emotional issues and wounds.

The goal of my business is to bring women to a place of deep and honest self-love, acceptance, and healing. I do this through various holistic methods that combine physical, emotional, mental, and also spiritual practises. Aroma Freedom Technique (AFT) coaching is one of the anchors of my program. This method combines coaching and aromatherapy, working through a stepped process, to unlock deep seated memories and beliefs, resolving emotional wounds and traumas. This technique is based in neuroscience and works with the science of memory reconsolidation, neural stimulation and amygdala switching. In common terms, this technique has the power to update and dissolve decades of old-learning patterns. It is based on psychological and neuroscientific principles.

I became a Certified Practitioner in this technique, and I have had some incredibly powerful experiences and shifts through applying this technique through my own healing journey. I have also seen some dramatic breakthroughs in my clients, using this technique in combination with the other holistic modalities, including Aroma Yoga®, Meditation, Yoga Nidra and Chakra Balancing.

The new programs on offer in 2021 (both in Studio and also online) will enable a deep dive into self-discovery and connection, acceptance and healing. I use a combination of holistic practices, (with an anchor in AFT) to dissolve old beliefs and emotionally charged memories that are keeping you stuck and stopping you reaching your goals and dreams. You will learn how to create and cultivate deep self-love and connection, and how to shift and align your body, mind and spirit from a place of dis-ease and stress, into a place of deep rest, health, vitality and abundance.

Min is leading her clients on their own journey of self-connection, healing, abundance and purpose.

MIN MELGAR
Essentially Well

M: 0401 596 270
E: essentially.well@outlook.com
W: www.essentiallywell.com.au

As a woman, wife and mother, prioritising your own self-care (especially your mental and emotional wellbeing in order to feel healthy and vibrant), is usually one of the last items on our 'to do' list. As someone who has experienced complete body illness and chronic dis-ease, I know too well the unravelling and devastating impact this can have on our own lives and loved ones.

Hi Beautiful, my name is Min Melgar, and my life's work is now dedicated to empowering women with emotional freedom, health and vitality. I teach you how to cultivate pure and fulfilling connections with yourself (in order to create complete wellness of the body, mind and spirit) allowing you 'the goddess', to BE and FEEL whole.

I walk alongside you and help you to reconnect with your true self - aligning and strengthening all aspects of your health. I support you to easily and effectively remove and release the mental blocks, trauma and negative emotional patterning that are keeping you stuck, and limiting your healing.

Every woman is unique and one approach does not 'fit all'. I work with you through my signature style of coaching, (which blends holistic modalities) providing you with a unique and tailored approach. Together we cut through the overwhelm, allowing you to take control of your health and begin living a life you love.

I am a Certified Women's Empowerment and Wellness Coach (Certified Coaching Federation), a Certified Aroma Freedom Practitioner and I am 350HR Diploma of Yoga qualified teacher. I have also studied and incorporate the teachings and philosophies of Louise Hay into my coaching and wellness program, alongside embodying a chemical free, low tox lifestyle. I own and operate Essentially Well, a Holistic Wellness Centre on the Sunshine Coast in Queensland, Australia.

OFFER:

I would love to offer a 20% discount off all Coaching programs for Feminessence® readers.

Simply reach out via the contact details above and mention Feminessence® to claim.

Activity

1. On a scale of one to ten (one being feeling unwell, to ten feeling super healthy, fit and full of life) where are you currently sitting on a scale of health?

____

____

____

____

____

2. What's the one area of your 'life of wellness', as it stands now, (physical, emotional, mental or spiritual), that you feel needs the most support and why?

____

____

____

____

____

3. Do you feel connected to your truth of WHO you really are and what YOU need to feel content, balanced and self-nurtured? If you do , do you regularly 'do the things' you need to keep yourself nourished? If the answer is 'No', do you need support finding out what these aspects are?

____

____

____

____

____

4. Do you currently have any regular health practises in place? These may include but are not limited too physical exercise, emotional wellness routines - including yoga, meditation, spiritual practices, self-therapy, taking regular time out for yourself etc?

____

____

____

____

____

5. What would complete wellness and vitality not only LOOK like, but FEEL like to you? Visualise it and describe it in detail?

____

____

____

____

____

____

ALDWYN ALTUNEY

Media Queen
Director/ Photojournalist AA Xposé Media

Inspiring gratitude
and good news

> '*Together, we can all make a difference*' – AA

I was born in Sydney's northern beaches in 1974 and grew up in a loving household where my beautiful European parents (Michael and Nelly) went above and beyond to ensure myself and my brother Nick had a great life.

I have Greek, Turkish and Ukrainian heritage. As all three countries have been at war with each other, I call myself the 'love child' now!

As a first generation Australian, I was bullied at North Balgowlah Public School from the age of six. Fellow students would pick on me because of my name, food I took to school and the clothes I wore. Anything they could pick on, they did.

As such, I grew up angry with the world and my parents and started rebelling from a young age.

Having European background, especially from Turkey where my parents grew up, the men would hang out with the men and women would hang out with the women. So my dad spent more time with my brother than me growing up and because of that, I felt some rejection from him at an early age. Soon afterwards, I began clashing with my mum.

My parents would say: "Why can't you be like your brother?" Nick was the studious, well-behaved one in the family. He thought scientifically (like my dad) whereas I was creative (like my mum). Not feeling like I belonged at home or at school, I ran away from home at age 13. Ironically, I was also the number one ranked Australian junior table tennis player at the time! I released my anger through the sport and developed a killer forehand smash.

At age 15, my dad was fed up with my constant rebellion to his strict rules. When I arrived home around 5am the morning after a Halloween party, he kicked me out of the home and said, 'You're not my daughter anymore'. I moved into a crazy household in Manly that day, with a drug-addicted drummer (whom I began to date), his alcoholic mother and drug-dealing sister. I began working two part-time jobs - earning around $5 per hour to cover my rent of $50 per week.

It was a complete party house with non-stop music and jamming until sunrise each morning. After six months of this, with my boyfriend lying to me and cheating on me, there came a turning point. I remember The Pretenders song Don't Get Me Wrong playing on the turntable and seeing my best friend at the time, kissing and cuddling my boyfriend on our bed.

I was 16 years of age and started bawling my eyes out. I called my mum in tears and said, 'I can't handle this anymore'. She said 'come home', which I did. Even though my dad was not happy about it initially, he gave me another chance and I ended up studying very hard with my brother Nick.

I had gone from Dux of North Balgowlah Primary School to failing everything in Year 11. I changed schools from Mosman High School to Forest High School at the start of Year 12. That was another turning point – changing my environment. I discovered 'the grass is not always greener on the other side' and started to appreciate my parents and family so much more. I ended up qualifying to do a Bachelor of Arts in Communication (Media) degree at the University of Canberra (UC) from 1992 to 1994.

While there, the role of Editor of the university newspaper, CUrio, became available. I applied three times before I was offered the position. I took the fortnightly publication from 24 pages to 48 pages and had 30 contributors, which I co-ordinated.

I became the longest serving editor at the paper and loved the power the media had to affect change in the community. I found the media was a great way to share my voice on what I felt were injustices in the world and ways to help make it a better place to live.

One of the first stories I wrote was an anti-duck shooting story with the headline Go and Get Ducked! I could not believe people were shooting ducks for fun and that it was legal in Australia.

I continued to write stories about issues that moved me in some way, including battery farming of chickens, female circumcision and stories about protecting the environment.

By the time I graduated from university, I received High Distinctions in my majors of TV Production and Photojournalism.

This was the start of what ended up being a lucrative career in the media for me. I went on to work as a journalist on TV, in radio and print media across Australia and internationally. Since then, I have interviewed stars including Charlie Sheen, Jewel, Vanilla Ice, Hugh Jackman, Russell Crowe, Cyndi Lauper, Debbie Harry (Blondie), Alby Mangels, Jimmy Barnes, Jimeoin and Mikey Robins, among others.

I worked as a journalist at The Daily Mercury in Mackay, Coffs Harbour Advocate, Queensland Times in Ipswich, Satellite Newspapers in Brisbane, Rave and Time Off in Brisbane, the Gold Coast Bulletin and Sun Community Newspapers (where I was a Journalist/ Sub Editor for five years).

I remember when I was working at the Sun in 2005, I attended an event with the National College of Business. The director Jon Mailer asked the crowd: "How much can you earn a week if you work from the head down?"

People said: "$1500 to $2000."

He then asked: "How much can you earn a week if you work from the head up?"

People said: "The amount is endless."

His next question was: "Wouldn't it make sense then to invest 10% of your income in your personal development?"

Everyone nodded and I had a striking realisation, aka an epiphany!

That year, I invested $7000 in my first personal development course in the Hunter Valley, NSW. To this day (16 years on), I have invested more than $500,000 in business and marketing courses, as well as many different modalities of personal development. This has been invaluable for the growth of my business and myself.

Since 2010, I invested in some programs with feminine empowerment mentors and started to work on my femininity - as I realised I was operating in a very masculine form with my strong work ambitions.

I attended women's retreats, weekend workshops and training to help me discover my essential power as a woman. We meditated, did yoga, chanting, dancing, women's circles, inner child healing and artwork, along with womb, shadow, breath, vertical core and conscious connection work.

This has helped me be open to receiving more in my life and inspired me to embrace the woman I am, as I am. It has also helped me trust women again - as I had trust issues from a young age with close female friends who turned against me for no apparent reason. Looking back now, I believe my girlfriends were often jealous of my success in table tennis and at school, although at the time I could not see that.

I have realised since 2010 that I do not need to lead my life in a masculine way and that it is just as important to receive as it is to give - and to trust myself more. The women's work with various mentors has helped me on this journey. The sisterhood circles I have participated in have been amazing for me to help me connect with my best feminine self and appreciate other women for how amazing they are.

My setbacks?

I fell pregnant in 2009 and miscarried naturally after nine weeks at age 36. That was very hard emotionally and I did a few women's workshops after that to help me heal.

I have had a few near-death experiences in life, including having a quinsy in my throat in 2014 - which flared up after emceeing for Colin Hay (lead vocalist of Men at Work who sang the famous song Down Under in 1980) at the Woodford Folk Festival on the Sunshine Coast.

A quinsy (also known as a peritonsillar abscess) is a rare and potentially serious complication of tonsillitis, which can kill you in a short amount of time if the swelling in the throat blocks the airways. I ended up in the Royal Brisbane and Women's Hospital on an antibiotic drip for three days over New Year's Eve 2014/2015.

This experience made me appreciate my life like never before. Hundreds of Facebook messages of condolence came through and I began to shed tears of gratitude for all the amazing people in my life. I wondered: "If I were to die, who would show up at my funeral? What kind of legacy would I leave? What do I want to create for my life?" Great questions which I often re-visit and reflect on.

When I first moved to the Gold Coast in January 2000, I never planned to stay there. My goal was always to live in America, so I rented apartments for the first two years. I remember in 2002, when I had to move on from one apartment in Labrador (the owner wanted to put her daughter in there) I had to look around for another place to rent. I was a very busy journalist at the time, so I decided to put an advertisement in the Gold Coast Bulletin to see if anyone had a suitable place for me to look at. I received a call from a guy called Lee, who said he had a place for rent in Main Beach across from the ocean. That sounded perfect, so I popped in to see him and the apartment and said I wanted to rent it.

At the time, Lee was a guy in his early 20s (looked like a surfy dude) and his young 18-year-old girlfriend was pregnant and lying on the bed.

I gave him about $1000 in rent and bond – that was more than my weekly wage back then – and he gave me the keys. When I went back to the apartment, there was rubbish all over the floor and benchtops, rotten eggs and food in the sink and the door to the balcony would not close.

I suddenly had this sinking feeling in my stomach. Something did not feel right. So I knocked on the door of the apartment next door and asked if they knew if the previous people were going to clean the apartment. They asked if I had spoken to the manager, which I hadn't. When I saw the manager, he angrily said: "Lee owes me three weeks in rent!" He was furious and so was I. Lee was not the owner! I gave the manager the keys and cried for about a week. I could not believe someone would do that or that I fell for such a con artist!

After that, I decided I would never rent again and thought, 'Why not buy my own house?' Soon afterwards, I bought a house in Southport. Now, 19 years on, I have fully renovated the house and still live there! Looking back, I am thankful for that experience. Even though the police closed the case, and I never received any money back, that situation inspired me to buy my house. I may have lost $1000 but if I were to sell my house, I would make more than $100,000.

I also believe in karma. What comes around, goes around 10-fold - and not necessarily by the same people who rip others off or do the wrong things! Karma is about cause and effect. What happens to a person, happens because they caused it with their actions. So if you want great things to happen in your life, do great things for others.

The divine feminine

I believe the essence of being a woman involves beauty, selfless love, purity, grace and dignity. Women symbolise virtue, inner strength, patience, resilience and fortitude. The feminine essence of a woman is honouring emotions and connecting with her intuition. The feminine embodies inspiration and masculine represents action, doing and completing tasks.

A woman who is constantly doing without taking the time to connect with her intuition can experience quick burn out, resentment, being unhappy and unfulfilled in life. This has partly to do with what women have seen their mothers and grandmothers go through. They have witnessed them being controlled and abused. Feminism was created in reaction to a collective trauma.

The wounded feminine is insecure, needy, co-dependent, manipulative, inauthentic, over-emotional and a victim.

The wounded masculine is controlling, abusive, aggressive, withdrawn, unstable, displays avoidance and over competitiveness.

The wounded feminine is co-dependent whereas the divine feminine is inter-dependent on the masculine - just like the divine masculine is inter-dependent on the feminine. Co-dependency means you rely heavily on someone else or your partner for your sense of self-worth, whereas inter-dependency means that you depend on each other to create a harmonious, balanced and loving environment. The divine masculine and divine feminine depend on each other to create a harmonious eco-system.

The divine feminine is intuitive, grounded, receptive (the essence of being feminine), considers herself worthy of receiving blessings, is grateful, playful, has boundaries, is empathetic, compassionate, vulnerable, magnetic, flows through life effortlessly, is trusting, creative, surrendering, open and authentic – and knows her worth.

The divine masculine is supportive, trusting, logical, present (focused), protective, confident, honest, accountable, has integrity, is humble, offers stability and security, has boundaries, does not judge, is deeply present and pro-active (takes initiative).

The black sheep

I have never married or had children. In saying that, my parents Michael and Nelly celebrate their 51st wedding anniversary in 2021 and my brother Nick and wife Angela have four children and have been together for 24 years.

Since the age of 38, I have been stressed about not being a mum or finding the 'right one' to have children with and start a family. I have been online dating for years and it was very hard emotionally - as there are many wounded people on dating sites. Now, at age 47, I have let go of being attached to wanting to settle down and have children with the man of my dreams. I have had a few false alarms and now my attitude is, 'if it happens, it happens and if it doesn't, it doesn't'. The important thing for me now is to be the woman of my dreams and then, the man of my dreams may show up.

I am very close to my parents now. They live in Bribie Island and I am on the Gold Coast. We see each other nearly every week and I take time out of my business to see movies and enjoy meals and conversations with them. My dad is 83 and mum is 77. They have had many health challenges and I realise the importance of making time for them in their ageing years.

As many of my friends have died before age 60, I realise the fragility of life and how important it is to make time for family and loved ones, no matter how busy business gets!

In the business world, I think it is important that women trust their intuition and bring love to what they do. This 'heart factor' can be missing with men who are often so driven by financial success and results. I believe with more female world leaders (who are in their divine feminine), we will have more peace in the world. Women often look to collaborate and create win-win situations; whereas with men (as hunters) in business, it can be like a battlefield!

Women often hold themselves back from success through naturally over-giving and not receiving enough. For women to be empowered, they need to be open to receiving and allowing success in their lives, without guilt. It's important that they truly love themselves for who they are and appreciate all they do and give to the world.

Passionate in business

I started my business AA Xposé Photography in 2002 on the Gold Coast after having a few small car accidents working late nights with a photography company in Brisbane.

After this, I thought, 'Why don't I just do this for myself?'

At the time, I was working as a journalist at the Sun Community Newspapers on the Gold Coast. When I left my position at the Sun, the business evolved into AA Xposé Media as people began requesting PR work, copywriting, video, graphic design, editing and media training services.

I did my first media training workshops in 2003 and had repeated calls for more. In 2014, I launched an online media training program called Mass Media Mastery, where I teach people how to get free publicity and mass media exposure.

I have members of my Mass Media Mastery media training program and membership site from all over Australia and several countries overseas now; including the Netherlands, South Africa, the US, UK and NZ. Most of them are small business people, authors, speakers and social entrepreneurs. Many I have never met in person - such is the power of online marketing!

I help people who have a great message, product or service to share it with the masses using online and offline media so they can build their credibility in the community, business, sales and leave a legacy.

I have had the opportunity to cover some amazing events including the HP International Circle of Excellence Convention, Harcourts and SWAP International Conventions, International Women's Day Festival, National Caterers Association Annual Awards, UDIA Gala Ball, Australian Institute of Fitness and National College of Business Graduation Nights, Gold Coast Business Excellence Awards, Entertainment of the Year Awards for Clubs in South Queensland, Indy Carnival of Colours, International Legends of League Corporate Golf Day, Gold Coast Airport Marathon and Blues on Broadbeach Festival.

There is never a dull moment with what I do.

In 2021, I also launched a Free Publicity Secrets online global workshop and annual program.

My ancestors are with me

I feel a strong drive and support for what I do from my ancestors. Scientifically, it is proven that we carry the DNA of seven generations. My great grandparents were two of the 30,000 Kulaks executed by Stalin's men in the Ukraine in the early 1930s. As part of the mass eradication of Kulaks as a class, they were hanged outside their house on their farm in Kiev.

My grandfather was in another part of the Ukraine at the time and started to speak up about it until his friends said: "Because you're speaking up against the government, they are coming to kill you now." He then ran away to Turkey and met my dad's mum, who was Greek.

I feel my ancestors are supporting me spiritually in helping others to speak their truth and speak up in the media. Some of my ancestors were killed, while others ran in fear of speaking up as a result of government control.

Advocate for animals & good news

A highly empathic person, I have always had an affinity with animals.

After years of seeing animal cruelty and feeling helpless to do anything about it, I founded the world's first Animal Action Day in 2007 to raise awareness, appreciation and respect for animals. I have since run 14 annual events, raising millions of dollars-worth of free publicity for different animal charities each year.

I have had depression over the years and had four friends take their own lives by the age of 45. As such, I am also passionate about promoting more good news stories in the mass media to help decrease depression and suicide rates worldwide, and lift people's spirits. In line with this, I founded a global Good News Day on August 8, 2018, and the monthly Global Good News Challenge via Facebook Live in June 2020.

A regular meetup group I run offering marketing advice is Mass Media Tribe and I co-launched the charity meetup group, The Gold Coast Business Laughter Club on August 30, 2018.

The elements of my media programs and how they work

In my media training programs, I cover my seven AWESOME steps to gaining free publicity. The AWESOME stands for:

A = Articulate Story

W = Work Angles

E = Elevate Profile

S = Startle Media

O = Own Power

M = Master Interviews

E = Explode Impact

I also train clients on social media marketing, including Facebook, Twitter, LinkedIn, Instagram and YouTube.

For clients who want all their media marketing done for them, I offer Media Star Packages where I uncover the gems of a client's story to develop media angles, press releases, photo shoots, pitch to the media, follow up with the media and run media training sessions, among other things.

I have the only media company I know of that guarantees media exposure. My goal is to help my clients go from being the world's best kept secret to being a star.

One of my great success stories is from my client, Aussie Mega Mall. The directors came to me in 2016 with no media coverage and, after a nationwide PR campaign, we achieved about 40 media spots (including on Channel 7 and Channel 9).

This led to them going from having 3000 online stores to 32,000-plus online stores and their business increasing 10-fold in the following three years. Now they are looking to launch internationally in the US, UK and NZ.

Future goals

I would love to have an offline studio TV show one day - to compliment my online shows on the Media Queen TV channel on YouTube. I love interviewing people and sharing their stories and wisdom. I would also like to start a global movement of more good news stories in the mass media than bad news stories. I believe this will make a massive difference in reducing depression and suicide rates worldwide. My wish is to have 1000 people participate in the Global Good News Challenge by the fourth annual Good News Day on August 8, 2021.

I am passionate about inspiring a positive world where people are optimistic and excited about their lives; a world where people love what they do and are excited about living life to its fullest potential. I want people to understand and appreciate the miracle they are as human beings.

Just by being born, they have beaten about one billion other swimmers to the finish line!

Every person is a miracle and has a unique gift and message to bring to the world. I want to inspire people to recognise and appreciate their gifts, to speak up and speak out about what they are passionate about and for them to create a ripple effect of change by being courageous and speaking their truth honestly and with integrity.

The few who run the world want people to live small lives and be slaves to the system.

Many people are brainwashed by the education and political system and don't even realise they are being brainwashed. I want people to wake up as individuals and combine forces with other 'awake people' in the community to affect positive change in the world - particularly in the areas of health, peace, sustainability and environmental protection.

"Be the change you want to see in the world", as Gandhi said.

And I say: "Together, we can all make a difference."

Here's to your media success! May you always make the most of every moment in this precious life and live a life that you and your loved ones will be proud of.

ALDWYN ALTUNEY

AA Xpose Media

M: 0409 895 055
E: aldwyn@aaxpose.com
W: aaxpose.com/freePRsecrets.com
W: linktr.ee/aldwyn

Aldwyn Altuney is a photojournalist with 37 years' experience in TV, radio, print and online media. Known as the 'Media Queen', she stands for truth, good news and animal welfare. Aldwyn hosts Media Queen TV on YouTube and co-hosts the Techwebcast podcast, which has had over one million downloads in the past 8 years.

Born in Sydney and based on the Gold Coast since 2000, Aldwyn runs 'AA Xposé Media', which offers public relations, photography and videography services plus the worldwide Mass Media Mastery and Free Publicity Secrets training programs.

Passionate about raising awareness, appreciation and respect for animals, she founded the world's first Animal Action Day in 2007. She has since run 14 annual events, raising millions of dollars' worth of free publicity for different animal charities each year.

Driven to promote more good news stories in the mass media to help decrease depression and suicide rates worldwide and lift people's spirits, Aldwyn founded a Global Good News Day on August 8, 2018, and the monthly Global Good News Challenge in June 2020. Regular meetup groups she has run since 2018 are Mass Media Tribe and The Gold Coast Business Laughter Club.

She has featured in 10 inspiring compilation books, many of which are international best-sellers.

Aldwyn was first interviewed at age 10 by the Manly Daily in Sydney as a number one ranked Australian junior table tennis player. At age 11, she featured on Cartoon Connection on Channel 7 and had her first media training session. She hosted her first radio show at age 13 at Radio Manly Warringah and represented Australia in table tennis from age 13 to 19.

During her Bachelor of Arts in Communications Degree (at the University of Canberra from 1992 to 1994), she became the longest serving editor of CUrio - the fortnightly university newspaper. Since then, she has interviewed stars including Charlie Sheen, Hugh Jackman, Russell Crowe and Cyndi Lauper.

She also loves performing in her comedy duo The Fiddly Gigglers, acting, playing ukulele, beach walks and body surfing.

OFFER:

Special for Feminessence® readers:

A private, half-price Media Consultation with Media Queen Aldwyn Altuney, where she uncovers the gems of your story, works on a media marketing strategy and finds newsworthy angles for you. Contact Aldwyn on 0409 895 055 or at aldwyn@aaxpose.com for details.

In the meantime, you can download my free guide on 5 Top Tips to Gain TV Xposure at www.aaxpose.com

Photography © Ricky Cornwell

Activity

1. What are you grateful for today?

____

____

____

2. What are you passionate about?

____

____

____

3. What achievements are you most proud of?

____

____

____

4. If you could change anything in the world, what would it be?

____

____

____

5. How do you want to be remembered?

____

____

____

LOUISE L. KALLAWAY

Author and 'Life Education' Specialist

Liberating Childhood
and adult time zones

> *'You have massive reserves of courage, emotional intelligence and intellectual resilience'* – LLK

Louise L. Kallaway has been fascinated by life processes since her teenage years. Her search to uncover and demystify the origins and power behind them has taken her more than 30 years. She now makes sense of life's jigsaw puzzle - with no missing pieces - in her empowering 'Life Education' series of books.

Her own life was difficult at times, but she felt aligned with the reasoning value of the Women's Liberation Movement and the changing face of that era.

"I am a baby boomer. I was entering my teenage years when the Women's Liberation Movement was getting started. It was a revolution ... a new consciousness! It was time for change! Women were openly demanding equality and respect, and a shift on a personal level to one of self-respect. We could no longer live the tiny lives of previous generations of women. We could no longer be silent or be silenced! Since World War II, we have been striving, proving ourselves, slowly taking ownership and responsibility for our lives as we began to realise our significant contribution and our importance in and to the world.

"I left school with my Leaving Certificate and started working full time at sixteen years old. This was not uncommon. There was an assumption that I would follow in the traditional role of secretary. I began my working life as a clerical assistant in a bank. I then joined an agency and worked as a temp. for a few years, learning the ropes of office systems and procedures. At 27 years old and without a degree - which was the new expectation - I became the Personal Assistant to the Chairman of Directors and the Company Secretary of a public company."

Louise had reached the top of her expected profession. "Where to from here?" she wondered.

In her personal life, things were not so rosy. She was having difficulty convincing her parents and the elders of her tribal family, that she should be allowed to make some minor decisions of her own – that she was no longer 'the child taking orders'. They were bewildered by her need for independence and labelled it as teenage rebellion. Regardless, Louise's need to explore more grown-up options continued. This was the first time that teenagers were openly demanding their right to be heard and to be taken seriously. "Why do they still think of me as a child … as if time hasn't changed anything?" she asked herself.

Still firmly ensconced in her childhood beliefs about her supporting role and her place in the world, she did not question this presumed position for many years; she simply accepted it as a given.

"This disruptive time co-incidentally planted the seeds of my curiosity into life processes and 'the system'. I began to question why, when I displayed signs of doing things 'all by myself' as a child, that my actions were applauded and encouraged, but a decade later, my teenage need to make minor independent decisions was considered rebellious? A giant question mark began to loom over life processes.

"Unbeknown to me at that time, this curiosity would become my life's work and the catalyst that would realise my innate ability to connect with my best feminine self. In fact, I did not discover my essential power as a woman until much later in life. The first inkling of my power began to blossom only after my research into life processes and 'the system' had identified some of life's major and best kept secrets. "How is this not widely known?" I wondered.

"In retrospect, there seemed to be a 'simpatico relationship'; a sense of camaraderie and cooperation between the Women's Liberation Movement of the 1960's, the new generation's protests and demonstrations and their vociferous demands, and those of my teenage years and 'our' unified need for respect and self-respect – all demanding a shift in power."

Alas! It was not easy for her traditional middle-class tribal family - who were living in their own generational beliefs and conservatism - to accept Louise's budding need for expansion and emotional independence. This added more vexation to her ambitious quest to understand life processes and why, what seemed like a perfectly natural progression to her, was seen as rebellious, even personal against them.

Eventually, when their controlling behaviours got too difficult to live with, Louise left home. She lived with her 'understanding' aunt and her family for a few months, before breaking ties completely with the tribal family and moving to the Gold Coast. She spent a year living and working there, coming to the realisation in her young life that if she felt strongly enough about anything, she had to overcome her fear and her 'need to belong' and be willing to stand on her own.

"I still believe fighting has no benefits and usually results in both parties digging their heels in even deeper, resulting in an impasse, and residual feelings of bitterness towards the other", she says.

So, what does Louise consider to be the essence of being a woman?

"To me, 'Feminessence®' is about affirmatively and consciously realising your enormous contribution on many levels. You are a complete and separate entity with your own special needs that only you can fulfil. You have massive reserves of courage, emotional intelligence and intellectual resilience. This allows your nurturing nature and your unique, intuitive self to engage with self-respect, adapting to the conscious, changing and maturing needs in your business, personal life and in society in general. We are the Masters of change and flexibility", Louise adds.

And what about the role of men in today's world? Where does that fit in with her views about women?

"I would like to introduce a new, powerful and different perspective, aligned with my research into life processes, that makes sense of the position of men today. Without a doubt, boys and men are struggling. I believe their struggle is similar to the 1960's Women's Liberation Movement. This movement was and is about changing our 'fit' in society. Today, men are trying to find their new 'fit' too – in a changing world that is demanding a new level playing field.

"Generally, men are coming from a belief that they were born into a higher position of unshared power. I believe their struggle begins with the presumed belief promised in the young, literal, and impressive minds of boys, tantamount to a traditional, generational belief system that is now being questioned. This belief system was confirmed through the observation of behaviours and attitudes shown by previous generations of women, men and society generally. Men today are trying to reconcile with their now seemingly demoted position, where women are striving for and demanding gender equality and recognition. Transition will always be a time of conflicting energies. Having been inducted into the notion of first position, this changeover cannot be easy for some men, especially when you consider that most have been brought up to think of themselves as the leaders, warriors and perhaps the breadwinners. They believe they are being separated unfairly from their promise or expectation, creating a sense of being 'ripped-off' and short-changed, leading to current stand-offs and frustrations. It is an image and a literal belief from childhood that is now conflicting with 'what is' happening, versus 'what was' their expectation.

"But, the women's movement is not personal against men per se – it is personal for women who are striving for a just and equitable share of power and opportunity. I think there is a huge difference in these attitudes and mindsets.

"I wanted to stay home for the first few years with my daughters. My husband was building his fledgling business. When my eldest daughter was around three years old, I re-joined the workforce as a part-time office worker. It was time to share my name 'Louise' with the word 'Mum' … to feel a sense of my own identity. It is amazing how good the human spirit feels when you are earning your own income, even if supplementary. Money and independence reinstate a sense of your own power and dignity – almost as if you are two different people.

"I happily accepted that I was the one who took care of the day to day needs of our family. Once our girls went to school, I started a mini business – 'Louise's Classic Glamour Services', which I conducted from home so I could 'fit in' with my daughters' school hours and their after-school activities.

"It wasn't until my daughters were in their late teens that I again felt a need to align with my maturing identity. I remember reflecting upon déjà vu memories of my teen years where my need for independent decision-making rose above tribal conformity and now, my need for independence and a sense of my own power were usurping the expectations of the institutions of marriage and motherhood. I remember verbally enunciating the words: "I want my life back!"

"I was always the support and had accepted that position all my life … until then. Shifting and balancing the power in my marriage was not possible. In fact, just like my teenage self, I had to leave. Although painful and isolating, it was again about fulfilling my obligation to myself – the adult rite of passage – rather than conforming with others or institutional expectations.

"A few years later when my life was more settled, my fascination and unfinished business with life's processes reappeared. I continued my investigation. Now, with some amusement I recall saying, even in my late fifties: "I still don't know what I want to do with my life!"

How does Louise think women can contribute effectively, in a business world that is still mostly run by men?

"It is not always easy to feel our feminine power and to feel comfortable living in that power, in a largely male dominated business world. Perhaps one way is to think of ourselves as complementary to men rather than in competition with them. After all, we are not men! We cannot be like them, think like them or behave like them while keeping the spirit of women alive and well. We have so many attributes, so many gorgeous qualities and we bring fresh new perspectives and softness into a world that still seems to be designed around masculine energy.

"Unlike men, part of our uniqueness is that we can wear makeup. Did you know wearing makeup can increase your pay rate? It has been proven. And … a bonus: women who wear makeup are listened to much more, seen as more competent and are taken more seriously. Perhaps that is one of our equalisers.

"Change takes time. Transition is never easy, there is a lot at stake. The women's movement is far from over. Some men will always see us in subordinate roles and will not share their inherited positions of power. It will take many generations to move into any kind of parity between genders. Once again, I think the best answer is to be as independent as possible, including independence in the business world. Co-incidentally there is a call for women to take more leadership roles in business and governments. We need flexibility in the workplace, especially when we have children. If this is not forthcoming, why would we want to work in rigid, unyielding structures?"

What does Louise consider the major contributor holding us back from success today?

"Learnt behaviours, observations and attitudes assembled in the first seven years of our lives create our 'unconscious' belief system aka our childhood model of life. This childhood belief system is carried forward into our adult lives via primitive, programmed automatic subconscious responses to childhood beliefs and current, similar childhood situations. Voila! We know exactly what to do, how to react, what we believe and how we feel. This system helped our primate cousins survive a hostile environment when we lived much shorter lifespans. Our inner child remains seven years old but our physical, intellectual, and emotional development continues as we mature.

"These primitive survival programs are 'dumbing us down' today! They are a major contributor, impacting and holding us back, as we live much longer lifespans. In other words, if we have not debriefed our childhood model of life, we will continue to live through our programmed automatic subconscious responses. These responses are coming directly from an out of date, literal, instinctual, powerless, dependent, idealistic and crude belief system.

"What behaviours did you see? How did the men in your life treat women - how did the women treat men? It is an attitude that is felt as much as it is seen. Children are instinctive and intuitive. You cannot trick kids on an emotional level – that is their language. They may not understand words, but they feel the tone of words, connect with facial expressions, and pick up on attitudes. These unconscious observations become enmeshed in childhood belief systems. Those beliefs form the foundations of our lives – colloquially known as our baggage – and create the conflicts we are seeking to resolve today in our maturing years.

"One of my major discoveries, and the one I base my books upon, indicating that we are living in two time zones, is the quotation from the ancient Greek philosopher Aristotle, C 384 BC – 322 BC:

"Give me a child until he is seven and I will show you the man."

"From the triumphant moment I added this final piece to life's giant jigsaw puzzle, with no missing pieces, I knew I could not keep this powerful and significant information to myself. I wondered: "How do I assemble all these pieces of information into a format with logical, reasoning value?" I was excited by the prospect of such a project! "Where do I start?"

"My 'Life Education' series of books have been written to shift adult awareness; to make sense of our lives so we can evolve. This series explores the two-time zones alluded to in Aristotle's quotation, explaining why it is imperative – and delightful – to work with our inner child and its model of life. On what do we base our lives, if not our childhood? Where do our feelings about ourselves, our fears, attitudes, beliefs and generational expectations have their origins? Separated from our foundations, we don't make sense. Becoming aware of our programmed automatic subconscious responses enables us to intellectually override powerless childhood beliefs and make decisions that are now current and work in our best interests, consciously refusing to live any longer as Aristotle's classic seven-year-old adult!

"It is a privilege and an honour to open our world to previously inconceivable possibilities. Liberating childhood and adult time zones, and breaking the cycle of 'stuckness' and powerlessness is a celebration of our empowered lives.

Louise's second book 'Defiance – Secrets of Your Midlife Crisis' received the honour and distinction of an Amazon #1 best-selling author award on 1st December 2020.

"I was in my sixties when I realised my purpose and put pen to paper! I really was a late bloomer, wasn't I? Now a slave to the quill, I have never been happier. Age should not be a barrier nor a deterrent to your passion. If there is something you feel strongly about and you have good health, I highly recommend you put your thoughts on paper. Every action begins with a thought and personal power begins when you take action. Be bold!

"I am passionate about beaming transforming light on the journey into our inner world. Disrupting the powerlessness of traditional thinking, connecting lovingly with our inner child and creating our 'dream-team' higher consciousness, no longer in conflict with our maturing needs, is significant. We can now unveil an enlightened, dignified and powerful adult."

Louise's 'Life Education' series of books gives people an opportunity to change their lives in powerful, positive ways. Her books offer exciting new concepts and insights, helping her readers to understand the likely reasons why they may be feeling disempowered and held back as maturing adults.

"With new understanding of the two time zones permanently operating in our lives, we are free to act from a place of immense higher consciousness and personal power."

She continues to receive glowing reviews and posts from people who have transcended their childhood belief system, and overcome the fear of stepping away from their innate and powerful 'need to belong' with its conformity expectations … possibly the maturing adult's greatest hurdle. They are now able to create their own identity, change their destiny, and live up to their highest potential. Expanding and honouring our predictable maturing needs is the adult's rite of passage.

These new, empowering realisations enable her readers to live authentically, fully attuned and appreciating their true Feminessence®.

References:

- Saint Louis, Catherine (2011) - 'Skin Deep. Up the Career Ladder, Lipstick In Hand', The New York Times. https://www.nytimes.com/2011/10/13/fashion/makeup-makes-women-appear-more-competent-study.html

- 'Wear Makeup, Increase Your Salary', Corporette, For Overachieving Chicks. https://corporette.com/wear-makeup-increase-salary/

- Zarya, Valentina (2016) – 'How a Little Lipstick Could Add Thousands to Your Paycheck', Fortune https://fortune.com/2016/05/19/makeup-more-money/

LOUISE L. KALLAWAY

E: louisekennett@bigpond.com
W: www.louiselkallaway.com

I was born in Melbourne, Australia. I have two daughters, six grandchildren and my cat Madelyn.

I have been fascinated by 'life processes' since my difficult teenage years. Before starting our family, I wondered *'Why do generational cycles repeat themselves'*, *'Where did these forces originate?'* and *'What was the power behind them?'* My quest has taken me more than thirty years, in my spare time.

I am now writing a series of 'Life Education' books to expose these programs and explain how survival intelligence, combined with our much longer lifespans are *'dumbing us down'* today. My books have been written to offer an alternative to the powerlessness endemic in traditional thinking ... to make sense of our lives.

When you understand that we have been living in two-time zones simultaneously – childhood automatic subconscious responses to current time, and fear, which is trying to keep us safe and contained in childhood comfort zones - this realisation stirs new and palpable possibilities for the maturing adult. Our feelings of 'stuckness' and powerlessness in midlife now make perfect sense and align with what is holding the unsuspecting adult back today. We have been on autopilot. Childhood beliefs are colloquially known as 'adult baggage'.

This is a massive shift in adult awareness. It's time to transcend our childhood fairy tales, expand our predictable maturing needs, honour our rite of passage and evolve. *Wilderness into Light.*

OFFER:

I would love to help you transform your life.

When you order my books directly from me, I will sign your copy and personally mail it to you:

louiselkallaway.com

Activity

1. Did you know adults are living in two time zones ... that we are on autopilot?

2. Do you know that primitive survival intelligence is 'dumbing us down' today?

3. Did you know that when you push childhood comfort zones you will get a fearful reaction?

4. Did you know it is your emotional independence that is your power base?

5. Did you know we must be willing to move beyond our 'need to belong' and its conformity issues if we want to evolve?

People are the biggest asset in life and in business; starting with YOU

> *'I listen to what people choose to say and make a note of what they 'aren't saying'* – CD

I grew up in an inner-city suburb in Sydney and was raised by my grandmother. Most people looking in considered it a 'rough' neighbourhood, yet I saw it as a diverse and accepting one; where people did not look at what car you owned, what clothes you wore or what your lineage was.

I had a somewhat privileged life and was raised by first generation immigrants who left behind a war-torn town to come to Australia. They arrived with patched clothes, a six-year-old son and a dream of having a better life. I have one brother and I am 10 years his junior.

Whilst my parents are from a very different, old school generation I would say they were progressive in many ways.

My father was ill for most of my childhood and his ailments continued through life. I was blessed that he had such a huge influence in my life. He passed away in March 2020. I only really got to know my mother as an adult, as she worked tirelessly to provide for our family with her energetic, 'can do everything' mentality.

As a child, I played cricket and football and was highly athletic; competing in all sports from gymnastics, to track and field, netball and hockey. You would often also see me with a skateboard. I was not quite the typical European, first-generation girl stereotype, and I do not recall accepting 'you can't' as part of my belief system – no matter who did what before me.

I don't recall looking for external approval.

I embraced challenges and I liked to test and try things. I guess in many ways I was a tomboy! I was happy to go against the grain if that meant working things out for myself to see 'What if?' I had a 'persistence/consistency' thought process in me. If I loved it once, I continued with it. I did not quit because someone told me it could not be done or that it had not been done before.

Being a girl and being raised by my grandmother, subconsciously perhaps, allowed me to be gentle and mindful of others. I looked after my grandmother as she aged. I even shared a bed with her. That was just a 'norm'.

I was taught boundaries, that revolved around respect, safety and in many ways about mitigating risk, being aware of your surroundings and who was in your proximity. I think I learnt from an early age how to gauge people and not judge; to see things from multiple angles.

As a female, I constantly look inwards to discover more about myself and why I do things or why I see things differently. I am conscious that I pay close attention not only to what I do but, to what others do and say. I notice patterns, choice of words, triggers, emotions and things that enable change to take place.

I listen to what people choose to say and make a note of what they 'aren't saying'. In doing so, I begin to understand what they really 'do' want to say but aren't there yet. In a world that is filled with 'noise', it is important to look beyond words, to see patterns, and to be aware of people's personal tonality and yes, especially **what they *do not* say.**

In my family life, I suppose I broke a few rules. We created a new path in respect to shared parenting, deciding that my husband was going to have a more active role. A career change enabled him to work around my career and our children growing up. While I worked 'corporate' hours, Bill balanced his work and was close to home, enabling him to do the children's drop off and pick-ups. However, I aimed to play an active role too, in that I was there for their major events, speeches, carnivals and Saturday sport. I was involved in numerous committees at my son's school whilst also establishing a new committee at my daughter's school.

Like everyone, I too experienced some challenges - personal and professional. I guess as I look back and laugh at some of them, I know that they contributed to shaping the person I am today.

These experiences are what drives me to share my story of 'going against the grain' because I want women to know that you can do things differently, and that it is ok no matter what others say or think. Being true to yourself, being authentic and not wearing a 'mask' (so that you fall in line with what others expect of you) is the key to living the life that you deserve.

I was a corporate mum that worked long hours and I had to do things so that they worked for me. That meant that I set boundaries, had a very tight diary system that was holistic across my personal and business life, especially as I travelled a lot for work. We had to establish strong communication skills, ensuring that we all knew who was doing what.

This also meant that I encouraged my children to be independent from a young age. They were taught to be involved in the kitchen – to chop and prepare food while standing on chairs at the age of four and to iron with a small portable iron. Yes, they made their lunches too!

We believed a shared journey involved everyone.

I know people looked at us and had their own perspective regarding what we were doing. I can assure you Bill had many eyebrows raised by his male counterparts, as did I. I had my fair share of guilt, however I kept focusing on where my values lay and that was to show our children 'they can' do it all no matter what.

Life for me is about 'showing' people how to – not telling them, and that started in our home as we showed our children they CAN DO IT. I recognise the power we hold within ourselves is far stronger than anything else, so I encourage people to reframe their mindset with self-talk and self-belief as this is the beginning of living the life that you deserve.

My company is called **Solutions2You.** I am a holistic Business Advisor. We help with strategic business guidance and people transformation.

I look at businesses and develop strategies for 'start-ups', small businesses, businesses that want to scale up and others that strive to work more efficiently. As an advisor, I mentor and coach business owners to take measured steps to achieve success. Often people are stuck with WHAT they want to do, and don't know where to start or how to do it.

I have a finance and counselling background, and have set up and run various businesses over the years. I work with a people focus, so I can support them to transition into creating their own independence. I help them take the small, measured steps towards having and running a successful business and living their purposeful life.

While my clients span from multinational business to start ups, I am passionate about seeing women and our future generation step into their true selves, so that they create the lives that they deserve. There is nothing worse than constantly thinking 'What else can I do?" and doubting yourself.

I have supported business owners to gain increases of 200% and improved productivity levels by 40%. But, the most satisfying thing I experience is seeing people believe in themselves again, despite others before me having told them 'it's too hard' or 'it's not the right time'.

Each person's journey is different. I do not have cookie cutter models. I work on a bespoke basis.

I understand the corporate world and create 'high level' strategies with 'helicopter' vision, but I also have the ability to break it all down to key milestones with measured steps, so you can work out what you need as you go.

Demystifying the unknown and taking the surprise element out of the equation is how I help people succeed. 'Navigating Your Path Forward' is a process where I dig deep into what you want, just as much as what you DON'T want. The key to understanding your drivers is to explore these before we begin. Knowing yourself and understanding your triggers, your patterns, your beliefs and of course your purpose (not just in business but in life) forms part of your 'WHY'.

Nobody in life should walk a path where they feel disenfranchised or dishevelled. They should have the opportunity to explore what is possible. No matter what lineage you are born into, or in what city or country, I want to create a space for you to explore 'What else?' and to be part of a greater purpose across the globe.

I think that taking the extra step to listen (so that I understand what I am hearing) helps me to be the person I am today, and this journey continues daily. As I have become more in tune with myself, I have learnt to see and hear beyond the surface and this allows me to connect with people at a level that evokes trust and creates change.

I have had clients say that they wish they had met me earlier, because they have wasted so much money with other mentors. They tell me that they just 'didn't know what they didn't know' and 'I don't know why I am sharing this with you – I have never shared this with anyone else? I feel like I know you and I trust you'.

What a privilege it is to work with these amazing clients! It is in these moments that change begins within them. They begin to see the power that they hold for themselves.

If you ask me to define Feminessence®, I would say it is the ability to celebrate the strength inside every female; being able to be assertive yet gentle and kind at the same time; to be compassionate and to share your vulnerability with those around you and truly know that by displaying these characteristics you are showing strength not weakness; to stretch yourself and know that your boundaries are limitless. Despite any adversity you may face, continue to strive forward lifting others around you.

I believe men are making changes that they want to see for themselves, and are becoming more receptive to supporting one another on an emotional level, however, woman are more comfortable being vulnerable with their peers.

Exposing your vulnerability as a woman is a strength, however, this may not be perceived the same way if you are a male. We need to create the space for everyone so that we can bring about balance.

As a woman, I see this type of transparency as a strength, as it shows that there is more to me than the professional person I am perceived to be. I see my transparency as a way to give others permission to be honest and open about who they are too. When we can be truthful with ourselves, we can move forward and make the changes that we want to see for ourselves. This extends to both genders.

Being different is what I encourage people to be. Differences bring about innovation and in these changing times, our differences will be what deliver success in business.

Have I faced challenges and obstacles along the way? Of course I have, but I truly look at obstacles as if they are an avenue to *do things differently.* No two individuals are the same, yet we all try to be or to do things like someone else. The incredible thing with a path is that you create it so that others can follow, but the difference is to do it YOUR WAY! This then becomes your path – one that you will show others so that they too can do it – **their way.**

I am aware that challenges bring about fear too and I have had fears like everyone else. Because of fear I have held back at times on sharing my voice.

Standing up and being different or going against the grain has not been a norm in my professional life (especially in the finance industry), however, I have learnt to recognise my triggers and acknowledge them so that I can move forward.

It is ok for others not to agree and to have strong opposing views, but equally so, it is important that you have a voice and that you share your thoughts too. Whilst we all like people to agree with us, it is important that we also understand that it is ok if they do not agree. What I have learnt as part of my discovery is to value that we can have different views. Knowing that you *can disagree* and that *it is not personal* – especially in business – is important.

This same philosophy applies in our personal lives. We can all have varying views. The choices we make need to align with our personal values and where we are on our own journey. In these instances, I look at 'intent'. When differences, obstacles or setbacks arise, it is important to look at the intent of where we all come from – and when we come from a good place, it means we are aligned but simply see things differently.

My advice to women is to *do things your way.* Go against the grain, especially if that is reflective of who you are. So often women believe that they need to do things the same way as their male counterparts (because that is how it has always been done). Perhaps this is correct, but I suggest that you revisit your thought process and look at who you are and what resonates for you.

Many people *don't know what they don't know,* so by showing them it CAN be done differently enables those around you to consider 'What else?'. This does not mean that they will agree with you, but you have planted a seed and given them an option. Being different, should not hold you back from staying *true to yourself* as you move forward. Presenting a different perspective will bring about change and that is how women can contribute differently in the workplace. Be the whole of you, the real you.

Why do women fear success? What holds them back? Fear, being judged and or rejection will continue to hold you back no matter who you are. When you succeed you have more 'eyes' on you so you become the subject of discussion. As a woman, I know that this is something that I was happy to step away from. In fact, I really did not feel the need to be seen – I did not need external approval and I did not need to be measured for any success.

I was acutely aware that I did things 'my way', somewhat differently to many women of my age so, 'standing up to shine' was another layer to add to the 'she is different' banner. I guess that had an element of fear attached to it, the fear to be seen!

Let me share a thought on how I realised that this thought process was remis of me. By holding back (as a result of the fear of continually been seen as different) I was not showing up to be seen by our future generation.

I realised along the way though that someone's negative feedback was likely not about me 'personally'. Everyone's experiences in life create a narrative for them and so the way I was being seen was through their lenses — their ideal world.

So, change the narrative — acknowledge the way in which the message is being received.

It is important to **never take rejection** or negative feedback personally. Accept we all have differences, and perhaps in that moment we felt judged, rejected or talked about by someone else - but it is one moment in time. That one moment may at a later stage be reflected upon and have a different outcome (whether you know it or not). Either way it's about them.

When you can accept this, you will be able to reframe your mind to set emotions, placing them to the side and separating the outcomes. This enables you to keep surging forward and to continue to embrace the differences you hold. Be who you truly are — transparent and the 'whole' of you.

I want to share a story with you.

I met this vibrant young woman named Helen when I was volunteering in orphanages and teaching English in Tanzania some six years ago. She was working in Insurance at the time and had some ideas about what she wanted to do. She wanted more from life but was not quite sure what or how. This is not an uncommon occurrence; I hear this often from women and our future generation who are disenfranchised with their current career.

She was searching for purpose and wanted to give back and serve others. One day she asked if I could look at a business plan she had written. I remember thinking at the time 'What a privilege to have someone that has stepped out of their comfort zone to ask for help!'

I wish more people could recognise that they can do just that. The fear of asking for help and being rejected prevents so many people from even starting.

It is also important to understand that if someone says 'no' it is not personal. It may simply be that they do not have the time, or they may not believe that they are best suited for you. It is very seldom (if ever) about you!

Secondly it is important to have 'skin in the game'. I see this as an investment in you. You need to want this for you – not for anyone else. Asking for help means that you are prepared to allocate the time to do the work and yes, that also means there is a monetary cost.

You will need to be consistent and to commit the time and cost so you can see the outcome.

Her quest to 'What else?' led her to apply for fellowships, grants, and in our discussions over the years she has found her way to being a mentor and supporting others to find their path. In her journey through these various stages, we have worked on new business plans, budgets, cashflows and strategies to align her values and establish projects that serve others. Helen is now also one of the Founders of Bora International and her journey continues to grow.

Helen's courage to ask for help and to trust in a path forward, seeking clarity and a limitless vision is what began my dream and has led me to where I am today.

'My end goal is to lift the baseline of where people start life across the globe so that they may live the life that they deserve!'- CD

'There are no limits except for those that we tell ourselves. Boundaries are there to be stretched. 'Dare to dream and you can achieve' this is a belief I want for you so that you may surge forward.'

- CD

CATHY DIMARCHOS

Founder and CEO, Solutions2You

E: info@solutions2you.com.au
W: www.solutions2you.com.au
f www.facebook.com/CathyDimarchosCoachSpeaker
instagram www.instagram.com/solutions2you_consulting
in www.linkedin.com/company/solutions2you-pty-ltd

Cathy Dimarchos is an award-winning Business Advisor and Mentor who is passionate about helping people leave a lasting imprint and creating paths that enable them to lead the lives that they deserve. As a professional advisor, consultant and motivational voice, Cathy dedicates her time to perfecting a combination of people, business and situational skills, delivering tangible business toolkits and solutions to clients from every imaginable background.

Like all careers, hers hasn't followed a predictable and straight-forward trajectory. She bounced between high-profile finance roles for big names like the Commonwealth Bank and sales orientated positions with companies like DK Learning, but it wasn't until she met two amazing, entrepreneurial men who gave her space to develop professionally and lead teams in new ways, that a light well and truly buzzed in her head. She needed to live in this world in a more complete way – one that allowed her the opportunity to open her eyes to different perspectives.

As time progressed, it became clear that Cathy wasn't cut out for a detached approach to numbers, figures and people. The GFC had arrived and swept thousands from stability; her clients were facing financial hardship, unacknowledged anxiety and mounting mental health issues. So, she changed the way she approached all three, studying counselling to further understand the machinations beneath the decisions and struggles she saw day to day in organisational roles. More than numerical support, Cathy goes beyond the product, or process, guiding her clients through their immediate needs, long-term options and real-time pain points.

Working across international borders, cultures and different perspectives for 18 months highlighted the importance of embracing her professional lives holistically. Collaboration, acceptance and the recognition of strength in difference became transformative – for both her, and for those she worked with. Her values took centre stage and business became honest and expressive. She believes that knowledge exchange leads to effective and sustainable outcomes.

Her calling is to support others realise their unspoken ambitions and step outside the comfort zones that regularly hold them back. Through empathy, strategic positioning and old-fashioned business skills, Cathy empowers people to establish healthy professional boundaries, think limitlessly and challenge norms, while rediscovering a curiosity about knowledge.

Cathy works with large corporates, SMEs and CEOs (as teams and individuals) to support them through change. Developing people to stretch their boundaries and deliver optimum outcomes is how growth is achieved in business. Her core mission is to support small businesses (in achieving their long-term goals) by providing strategic business advisory while developing future leaders to break through traditional thoughts and beliefs.

Through her upcoming book "Same People, Different Vision" (which will be released in the second half of 2021) Cathy Dimarchos is adding yet another key element to her purpose of lifting the baseline across the world and developing the leaders of tomorrow.

OFFER:

Do you want to walk on the numbers runway like a pro? Get in touch for a special free 'Numbers Consultation' (valued at $275).

Book in with me at solutions2you.com.au/feminessence

If you're struggling to put it all together, I would be more than happy to help. It's my passion to show women how they can do this on their own. Contact me to get my free tutorials or for a full 1:1 session!

Photography © Images by Zahrina Robertson Photography and Video

Activity

Put your Numbers on the Runway.

Numbers are no longer a 'Man's game'. Until today nobody has had the courage to make Budgets and Cashflows look sexy but I am here to change that!

I will show you how knowing your numbers can bring you the confidence to walk down the business catwalk with your head up high.

When it comes to numbers, your bank account is a good place to start but it doesn't tell you the whole story. That runway is not just a paper game but your whole future unveiling itself in front of you, waiting for you to step into the spotlight.

Get your transactions out of your bank account, open your spreadsheet and let's introduce your top models:

- **Model #1 - Your Expenses**
  Start by making a list of your recurring expenses. Think subscriptions and regular fees - things that you can (and should) plan for. Get them on the runway!

- **Model #2 - Income Sources**
  Next step is to look at where your income is coming from. Your products/ services need to make it onto this spreadsheet. Make a note of how much money is made from each of them — know your margins! (Don't forget your promotions and sales.)

- **Model #3 - The star of the business: YOU!**
  This is where you get your power from. Forecasting your goals and knowing how much you need to sell to cover your expenses and grow your business. So, get the confidence to make smart decisions.

Make this real and take control.

From tomboy people pleaser to finding Feminessence®

> *'You deserve to live a life with passion and purpose!'' – KS*

Matchbox cars and boys' games were a big part of my childhood.

As I have two older brothers, I learnt to play boys' games, as the boys were certainly not going to play dolls with me! I was a real tomboy, and my feminine side was pushed aside and really did not surface until later on in my life. Adjusting myself to fit in with others was my norm, and it ensured that I always had someone to play and connect with.

I was a sensitive child, feeling things deeply. I would even cry when the grade one teacher got annoyed at the other children, even though it was not directed at me. I did not have the emotional intelligence to feel comfortable with my feelings and to understand what those emotions were trying to tell me, so I suppressed them. In fact, over time, I became a master of pretending that everything was ok and suppressing my emotions. Often saying 'Yes I'm fine' when clearly, inside I was not.

In grade four our family moved for a year to the Southside of Brisbane and this was the start of a year of bullying for me. My bully knew how to manipulate me to stop me from speaking out about her behaviour. It took until adulthood before I would learn to handle manipulative and controlling behaviour. I am now passionate about teaching children and adults the emotional intelligence, the skills and resources needed to handle people and situations - skills I wish I had when I was being bullied in grade four and again in high school.

My parents, like most parents, worked hard to create a better life for us children than their own. Both of my parents were exposed to elements of violence in their childhoods. Mum was a hands-on mother who spent a lot of time and energy helping us to explore our world. I learnt early in life that if I did not mold myself to be and do whatever someone else wanted, I would not connect with that person. My emotionally distant and critical father cemented that belief. I wanted to feel harmony in our family so badly, that I became the peacemaker. I learnt to avoid uncomfortable conversations, feelings, situations and potential conflict. I felt I was always trying to keep everyone happy and positive. Avoidance and distraction were my tools.

With low self-esteem I had created a pattern of always putting the needs of others before my own; in fact, I didn't even really know *what* my innermost needs were. These were the seeds of 'co-dependency' and 'enabling' that started to manifest themselves in my life. I was so busy molding myself to be whatever somebody else wanted me to be; busy trying to please everyone. I was the perfect example of a people pleaser, sacrificing my time, energy and resources for others.

This was carried through into my first marriage and the raising of my two beautiful sons. I did not yet understand that self-care was of fundamental importance to my becoming a full and complete person. I wanted to be liked by others so much that I adjusted my expectations and needs to meet the needs of everyone else. Healthy boundary setting was not my strong point especially, in intimate relationships. I did not really know what my boundaries were. I did not always feel comfortable with how the behaviour of some others affected me, but I could not articulate why I had those uncomfortable feelings, let alone set an appropriate boundary for them.

While it is common for mothers to sacrifice for their family, I had lost myself in placing my family's needs always ahead of mine, and working tirelessly to please my then narcissistic husband, with his never-ending demands. Consistently putting other people's needs and wants ahead of my own meant my desires were constantly being moved down the ladder of importance and priority to accommodate others. This was, of course of my own doing.

With little emotional intelligence, I did not understand 'Why I did what I did' nor the emotional games that people play, I fell victim to their manipulation. And with conflict avoidance patterns driving my behaviour, giving in to keep the peace was a recurring theme.

What I didn't know then was that 'peace at any price is no peace at all'.

Confronted with a strong and forceful person with powerful views and opinions, I was easily intimidated. I was quick to assume that my opinion must either be wrong or, because I did not want the conflict of standing up for myself or my truth, I was quick to shut down and did not voice any opinion at all. I struggled in places of conflict or tension to even speak. My voice box would close and speaking up became hard to do. I have now faced that fear, and after joining a safe environment of public speaking at 'Toastmasters', I can now speak in public and express my opinions to an audience. I wish I acquired the skills earlier. I applaud environments where healthy debates are encouraged inside and outside of the family unit. I encourage people to recognise how to spot the toxic and unsafe behaviour of others and how to set healthy boundaries.

My fear of conflict led me to avoid it like the plague. Not surprisingly I had married someone to fight all my battles for me. The only problem was that I was losing all the battles in the relationship and he was winning them all. I was co-dependent, playing victim and waiting for someone to come and save me. I finally realised that that rescuer was going to have to be me!

Nobody else was going to save me or fight my battles for me. It was time to stop being a passenger in my life, and to step into the driver's seat and take control. It was time to find my voice.

Eventually I started sucking up psychology and started to understand why people do what they do. This was the turning point in my life of empowerment and personal development. I began to understand why I was the way I was. I started to understand the beliefs and values that I had collected in my childhood (as we all do) were driving who I was today and whilst those behaviour patterns had served me once, they were no longer serving me now. It was time to start examining those childhood coping strategies as these were the cages that kept me locked in co-dependency and unfulfillment.

I eventually left the toxic relationship and started on my journey to get to know me; to find out who I really was. I was not just an extension of my then partner and the mother of my boys. I had buried my needs, wants and desires under a life of self-sacrificing for others. I needed to find out what brought me joy and happiness; what lit me up and got me excited about life. I had to create a life for myself that I could be enthusiastic about. I needed to find my passion!

What I found was that I enjoy having deep and meaningful conversations about life; becoming a Life Empowerment Coach was a perfect fit. I love to empower others with the knowledge, wisdom and understanding that I once did not have. Because 'We don't know what we don't know'. I know what it is like when everything in your life is not 'all together' and I know the steps to get there – I have been there, I know the path out. I have a mission to support women to gain insight into why they are the way they are and to give them an understanding of what beliefs have been driving their lives and decisions for

so long; examining what is working for them, what is not working for them and supporting them as they break free of the childhood coping strategies that are no longer serving them. I give them the clarity, confidence and courage to create a life that they can get excited about.

I love the expression 'You're not stuck. You are just committed to a behavioural pattern that served you once but is no longer serving you. Time to break free of the past beliefs and behavioural patterns, and learn some new patterns', because the coping skills you acquired to survive childhood are not the skills that will allow you to thrive later in life.

I believe we are drawn to people and situations where we need to learn a lesson, to hone our personality and skills, and to improve the areas in our life where we are not strong. We all have strong and weak parts to our personality. We all have different lessons to learn in life. If we can learn to stop worrying about what is happening to us and start to look for the lessons that circumstances are trying to teach us, we will move forward into a happier and more fulfilling life.

My mission in life is to empower others with the knowledge that I so wished I had had earlier in life.

I have finally learnt the difference between enabling and coaching others to improve their lives. Where once I thought I was helping others, I was in fact enabling their unresourceful behaviours and not allowing them to feel the full consequences of their decisions. We are free to choose to do whatever we want in life, but we are also responsible for the consequences of our decisions and actions.

The story of my life had been that in order to avoid judgement and conflict I shut down or 'played it small' to maintain some sort of control and connection. I finally got sick of playing it small, being bored, unfulfilled and not being in control of my life. It was time to dream big. Time to take control and get in the driver's seat of my life and start to create a life that I could get excited about. I want to leave a positive legacy of empowerment for all women. The support and guidance that I so desperately wanted and needed in my life, is now what I offer to my clients.

My heart sings when my clients - whether through my monthly self-care workshops, overnight retreats, online courses, webinars, podcasts, or one-on-one coaching - find the clarity, confidence and courage they need to create a life that they can love.

It is a thrill to see the shame and self-judgement lift when my clients start to understand why they are the way they, are and forgive themselves for the decisions and choices they made in the past with their limiting knowledge, skills and understanding. It was similar to when I watched Oprah Winfrey, her guests and audience get 'light bulb' and 'ah-ha' moments. I also love to watch my clients find these gems of understanding that will support them moving forward into a better life.

As a Certified Practitioner in TimeLine Therapy, Matrix Therapy, Neuro-Linguistic Programming, Hypnosis, Mbit Coach and Emotional Intelligent Teams Program, I have extensive experience in re-programming behavioural patterns that have us running on autopilot and stop us from achieving our fullest potential.

Through gaining a deeper understanding of themselves, I guide women to break free of the anxiety, depression and limiting beliefs that are no longer serving them.

My passion is to see women become the truly capable, independent superwomen that they are – my wish is to leave a legacy of empowerment to all women!

I believe that every parent loves their child and is doing the best they can with the skills they have. Sometimes those skills are not enough. We do not choose which family we are born into, but we are responsible for healing any emotional past baggage that we carry. Let's stop the generational dysfunction from being passed on from generation to generation. Let the past emotional pain stop with you and this generation by healing our own emotional wounds.

Women in our Australia have been brought up in a patriarchal society and have had to fight for equality. We have come a long way but women are still at a disadvantage to this day. I believe that if we want true equality in the workforce, we need to see childcare as a family issue and not just a women's issue. I also believe that the first seven years of a child's life are where we formulate our beliefs, values and behavioural patterns and that it is critical to create a society structure that supports our developing children, parents and workplaces. The foundation of stability, love, support and nurturing is paramount in creating a happy family unit as well as a safe, supportive and inclusive community in the future.

We have measured, acknowledged and revered intellectual intelligence for a long time. It is now time that we start to acknowledge the incredibly important role that emotional intelligence plays in everyone's life - inside and outside of the work environment. It's time that emotional intelligence was taught in all schools.

We have been living in a very profit driven, competitive, somewhat masculine world for some time now. It is time for our community to have a more collaborative feminine approach to how we run our workplaces and our society. We need to make more conscience-based decisions that are less profit driven and based more on sustainability for all. When one of us wins – we all win. My motto is that 'If it is not a good deal for both of us, it's not a good deal. Period.'

I believe that women do not have to compete with men. Both men and women bring different sets of skills to the table. We need to have an environment in all workplaces where we have diversity of sexes, cultures and beliefs because we all bring our own unique set of skills to the table. I remember raising two boys, and being the only feminine voice out of the four of us and having the belief that my perspective was 'just mum' and not a women's (feminine) perspective. We need to acknowledge that each and every perspective is valid and worthy of consideration.

As the nurturer of babies and life, women bring a unique set of qualities with our feminine energy and perception. If we can learn to tap into our masculine (strong, single-minded, focused and competitive) side we can also bring forward the feminine side (with our sensitivity, supportiveness, gentleness, compassion and sense of co-operation) for a more inclusive and harmonious life for us all.

I want to see a world where both men and women can have dreams and desires for their lives, and both have the capacity to fulfil those dreams. We need to create genuine equality, unlike the patriarchal society that I grew up with, where women were only there to serve and fulfil the dreams and aspirations of the men. I believe this will create a better life for both men and women when mothers and fathers share an equal and connected life with their children and their community; where both masculine and feminine energy is celebrated as a natural part of both men and women.

I finally know who I am; what makes me happy; what makes me tick. I feel empowered. I'm in the driver's seat of my life. I have dreams, aspirations and goals that I am excited about. I have surrounded myself with amazing people that I respect and admire, that inspire me to be the best version of myself and motivate me to grow and achieve, that are immensely talented, supportive, positive, generous and kind. I want, encourage and support my clients, family and friends to create a life that is fulfilling. A life that has passion and purpose, that they too can get excited about.

Empowered is how I now feel about myself and my life. From years of allowing others to control and direct my life I am now fully in control and surrounded by supportive people. I am finally letting go of the limiting unresourceful beliefs that held me back for so long.

I know what works and doesn't work because I have been there. I can support and guide other women away from feeling stuck and directionless to a life of empowerment, purpose and passion. I can give them the clarity, courage and the confidence to create an amazing life.

"You're not stuck. You are just committed to behavioural patterns that served you once but are longer serving you. Time to break free and learn some new patterns!" - KS

OFFER:

I would like to offer Feminessence readers a 20% discount on my Empowerment Coaching Program

This is a 9 week one on one program to support women to have the courage, confidence and clarity to create a life that they can get excited about. This discount will also apply to my self-care workshops and on-line courses.

lifechoicescoaching101.com/work-with-us/#empowerment

Photography © Rebecca Taylor Photography and Soul Echo Photos

KERRI SPEYERS

Life Choices Coaching

M: 0405 971 871
E: info@lifechoicescoaching101.com
W: www.lifechoicescoaching101.com

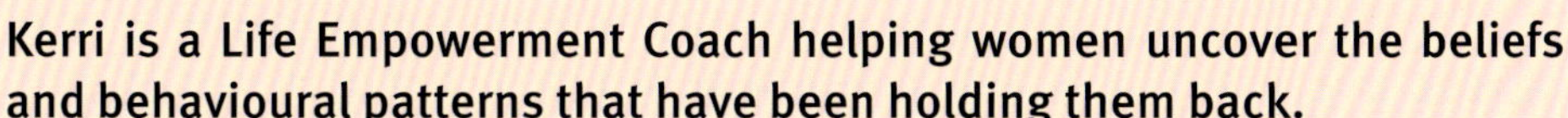

Kerri is a Life Empowerment Coach helping women uncover the beliefs and behavioural patterns that have been holding them back.

For over 35 years Kerri has been working to educate and support others through the Medical and Education system, and working with mainstream students and special needs students, as well as raising two sons.

She creates a supportive, safe and nurturing space, helping her clients uncover and clear the limiting unresourceful beliefs and behavioural patterns that served them once but that are not serving them now. Breaking the patterns that were holding them back and empowering them to create a life they can get excited about. Kerri believes that the coping strategies that helped her clients to survive childhood may not support them to thrive in adulthood.

People come to Kerri as she has been there herself and knows what it is like to be 'stuck'. She knows what works and what doesn't work, and creates a safe place to open up and create transformational lifelong positive changes.

Kerri is passionate about empowering women to create their best life by helping them to understand 'why they are the way they are'.

Kerri is a qualified Life Coach, certified in Time Line Therapy, Neuro-Linguistic Programming (NLP), hypnosis, Mbit Coach, Emotional Intelligence Teams Program and EDISC program.

Working with Kerri through her Life Empowerment Package, Self-Care Workshops, Online Courses, Podcasts and Retreats, is about understanding the missing resources and life lessons you needed, and breaking those limiting beliefs and behavioural patterns to allow you to create powerful, lasting, positive changes for a better life.

Activity

Some questions for you to consider:

1. Are you living a life that excites you?

2. Does what you now do in your life either through your work or your other interests get you excited to get out of bed and pursue it?

3. Have you learnt to forgive yourself and the decisions that you previously made with your life?

4. What is the legacy that you will leave in your life and are you proud of it?

5. Are you surrounded by people that you respect and that inspire you?

Finding your identity as a woman

> *'I am Strong, I am Invincible,
> I am Woman'* – HR

I grew up with a mother who sadly, had severe mental health problems, and alcoholism was her coping mechanism. She was in denial about both afflictions. My father was a very anxious, stressed man and he really worried about what other people thought of him. He also had a raging temper! They both lived quite isolated lives with few external friendships.

My earliest memories as a child involved my ability to be independent. I was a young girl with maturity well above her years – and this was my survival mechanism. When I think back now, I have always had a shield around me. I guess it was my shield of protection - to help block out any negative energy around me.

My parents did not really understand or involve themselves in our further education, so they had no expectations of us becoming doctors or lawyers. In the 80s, as a woman, you were most likely to become a secretary, a teacher or a nurse. Amongst my friends, it was the norm to find a nice man, get married and raise a family.

When I was 12, I started working at a local nursing home, doing the laundry, cleaning and evening cooking. I made around $12 per hour, which was not too bad for a 12-year-old! From the moment I started working I began looking after my own needs - such as paying board, buying my own clothes, movie tickets etc.

As I look back, I can laugh at myself now to see how clever I was as a child, having such a responsible head on my shoulders and thinking that I had my life all worked out. I always took responsibility seriously!

At the end of Year 10, I made the conscious choice not to continue on at secondary school. I felt annoyed that we learnt nothing of great substance, and it felt like a waste of my valuable time. So, I enrolled myself into Secretarial College, applied for study allowance, and paid for the rest of my tuition from my little nursing home job.

What a wonderful year that was! I was with like-minded young women who wanted to learn -and learn we did.

Now, looking back on my childhood, it allowed me as a woman to discover many valuable life skills such as independence, resilience and growth. I believe my independence has given me a strong sense of who I am and what I can achieve as a woman. I am head-strong, yes, but soft in my nature. My curiosity has allowed me to achieve so much in my life. I set goals, visualise, grow and go after my dreams.

When I was working in corporate management, I remember that I had reached a point where I just felt that I was no longer connected to who I was. I felt trapped, so I stopped nurturing my inner wisdom and my empowerment. I now know that I need these energy elements in my life to be in flow with who I truly am as a woman.

I have enormous compassion for women who feel stuck and want to find happiness in their careers and lives; women who cannot express how they feel in their heart and are living their lives by putting up a wall of fake perfection. Women have several natural talents and strengths within themselves, which many are not even aware they have!

It has not always been an easy ride. When I was 24, my husband and I experienced the emotional trauma of losing our first baby girl, Tamieka. She was stillborn at 39 weeks on Valentine's Day. We lived interstate, away from family, but we had some amazing friends to help us through this very sad time. If you had asked me the year before, how would I handle the loss of our baby girl, I would have told you it would be impossible, and I would not be able to cope at all.

However, with my very supportive husband, we worked through our emotions together. It was tough, very tough. Our friends and family were understandably distraught by our loss. Some found it very hard to come to terms with it and avoided speaking to us.

By nature, I am an empathic person and have a strong emotional awareness of others' feelings. I felt very concerned that those closest to us were hurting so much. To help our loved ones through the grieving process, I openly talked about our experience (not morbidly but lovingly) to show our friends and family that we were doing ok and did not want them to worry. Together we would heal. But behind closed doors, my husband and I were heart-broken and cried for our baby daughter.

Reflecting now, I realised I had found an inner strength and energy that I never thought would have been possible. I found my path to healing through connection and learning about who I really am as a woman and how mentally strong I could be.

What do I think the essence of being a woman involves? I always think of the lyrics in Helen Reddy's song 'I am strong; I am invincible; I am woman'. I believe that sums up the Feminessence® of being a woman. It is about being a woman who is in tune with her emotional awareness and energy; a woman who is proud of her femininity and owns it; a woman not afraid or shrinking down but rising to the top, on an equal footing with men. This is an empowered woman!

Equality has come a long way and still has a way to go. However, it is not only men who need to adjust their way of thinking about a woman's role in life. Women also need to play a part in bringing their authentic self to the forefront by not masking their feelings, ambitions or needs. We need to speak out and communicate how we feel! As a woman, we have it within us to be empowered in our life and our career. We need to stop playing small just to please everyone else or stay unseen.

Women are not the weaker sex. We just process our thoughts and how we approach matters differently to men, bringing about unique perspective and outcomes. But we need both man and woman to embrace each other's differences; to demonstrate acceptance and equality for both sexes.

I am uplifted hearing woman speak about their ambition and dreams. Sometimes they may need a little guidance to get them there. But they are women. They are strong, and when they put their minds to it, they can do anything to achieve their goals and dreams.

We had our two daughters in the early nineties, and back then it was quite common for the mother to say at home, raising her children and looking after the household whilst the father went to work. When our eldest daughter turned two, I missed having the stimulus of a job, but I did not want my daughter to go to day-care. So, I started a resume writing business from home. I worked around my daughter's nap and bedtime. It was the perfect solution for us.

Because of a complicated pregnancy, I closed my resume writing business. So, when our third daughter was born, I again enjoyed being a stay-at-home mum until she turned two. But this time I went back to study and studied Business Management and Accounting at night. My husband and I would play tag team, and as I went off to school he would feed the children and put them to bed. In our 31 years of marriage, we have always worked as a team. Sure, we have our 'assumed responsibilities' in our household, but it does not mean that they are solely our responsibility. We step in for each other when we can. There are certain household chores that my husband does better than I can, and vice versa. We balance each other's strengths and weaknesses out.

I think women bring their own unique set of skills and strengths to a business, just as men do. It is important for a business to have a diverse workforce of people who are different in thought and experiences, as this brings innovation and growth. A woman's special contribution and her attributes come from how she thinks and the natural insight she possesses. Women are also great multi-taskers, so often woman can run their business and a household with children. Women are natural connectors and have communication skills, which adapt intuitively to their customers' needs. Research states that women are generally more time productive in business than men, even though we like to chat a little more than our male counterparts!

I established Identity Empowerment Coaching in 2019 after a corporate redundancy. Shortly after my position became redundant, I flew to Melbourne to visit my mother. As my laptop bag was being checked, the nice customs officer asked what I did for work? Without giving it a second thought, I responded that I was an Operational Area Manager and travelled for work.

Why had I said that? I suddenly realised that I had lost my professional identity. In effect, I was in DENIAL and felt confused about who I was and how I fitted into my own life!

My identity had become tied to my career!

On the flight, I thought about how many other women have felt the same after a redundancy, or who are not living their true identity; women who felt stuck and wanted more meaning and authenticity in their lives; women who sought more happiness, freedom and the ability to make an impact in their career and personal life.

From that moment, my vision was for every woman to have Identity Empowerment; to know who they truly are, that they are worthy of success and they can do anything they put their mind to. My business - Identity Empowerment Coaching was born!

I felt a surge of energy and drive. A light bulb went off in my head and I knew in my heart I had found my 'Y'. Little did I know I was about to embark on a journey of my own *self-discovery and empowerment. I only wish I had taken control of my feminine power sooner!*

Upon starting my business, I knew I wanted to work with women who are introverted; women like me, who have felt stuck for too long; women who feel that they are simply not being fulfilled by their career or living to their full potential; women who have not found their 'Y' and are still searching for it; most importantly, women who need guidance and nurturing to learn how they can empower themselves to live the lives and have the careers they wish to have.

My Feminessence® is to empower as many women as I can, to help them soar high by learning the steps they can take to reach their full potential in their career and their life, whether they want to work for a company aligned with their values, run their own business, or to achieve other personal life goals.

I am a firm believer that when women put their minds to a plan and goal, they can achieve great things.

I focus my Career Counselling and Personal Development Coaching approach on my clients' strengths and self-awareness. I help women to re-energise and relaunch their careers, to choose careers, which align with their strengths and authentic selves, by supporting them through a journey of self-awareness, self-confidence and career counselling strategies.

All women should be in careers, which align to their values, passion and energy. They should be doing what makes them happy and feeling in their natural flow.

At Identity Empowerment Coaching, each of our programs is customised and designed to guide our clients through their unique challenges - whether it is around mindset and personal development, re-energising their career, re-entering the workforce or transitioning into an alternative career path (including the pathway into entrepreneurship). A complimentary 20-minute coaching strategy session helps my clients to determine if they are ready to invest in themselves, work through their career goals and ambitions but most importantly, if they are ready to stop making the excuses, which are holding them back from flourishing in their career and life.

Identity Empowerment Coaching helps support women to harness their feminine energy and embrace who they are and want to be in their lives and careers.

As an example, one of my clients was experiencing a hostile work environment whereby she was not being acknowledged for her contribution, and her ideas regarding business growth and development were being ignored. My client felt unappreciated and not at all happy in her job. She was also experiencing some age discrimination within the workplace.

As an aside, I am very passionate about people being treated with respect and fairness in a workplace. We all have something important to contribute, no matter our age.

As we worked together, I was able to spot the strengths, which energised my client; those that she performed well and used often. We also worked through self-discovery and self-reflection, and practiced mindset and confidence building exercises. My client's realisation was that because of her internal fear, she was staying in a job, which did not align with her values and worth, stating that it made her feel sick and apprehensive to go to work each day.

I was able to help her achieve a wonderful outcome. She made several breakthroughs and one, which excited her. She realised she loved to write and wanted to pursue her career in writing. Since then, my client has written professionally and has also worked intensively on her personal development, changing significant aspects in her life and embracing her 'identity empowerment' to make change happen.

Most of my clients suffer from feeling debilitated by thinking that their skills and capabilities to perform the job are not good enough. I have experienced this myself – and it is affectionately known as 'Imposter Syndrome!'

Another one of my beautiful clients manages her own company but was struggling to advance her business because of inner voices of self-doubt. She felt she was underqualified to provide the services she was offering and was comparing herself to other women in her industry, causing her to hold back from 'showing up' in her business and being seen. We went on a journey of self-discovery to find her strengths. Once my client could see how she could utilise her strengths she began to feel more confident about her ability, this allowed her to change her way of thinking. She loves connecting and empowering people, and prior to COVID-19, loved to network. However, time away from networking had seen her lose her self-confidence, and she doubted her own ability.

We worked through her self-limiting beliefs and she is now making wonderful progress in her business, simply by changing her mindset, believing in her ability and knowing how to draw on her natural strengths by bringing out her authentic self. My client is now feeling more confident about her ability to serve her clients and promote her business with confidence.

It makes my heart sing when I know that I have helped to uplift a woman, to show her that if she is feeling unsettled there are options, and she can become empowered to live and work as she chooses - to help her take bold and inspired action so she can grow personally and professionally.

For too long, women have struggled in unhappy careers and are too afraid to speak up. They feel obliged to stay in the same career for either family stability, being comfortable in an environment they know or for fear of trying something new. This can have a detrimental effect on the self-esteem of a woman.

After going through my own personal transformation, it saddens me to know that there are many more women who are living without knowing what is next for them, feeling lost in an empty void and confused, also scared of taking that next step. Women do not always recognise their own value and what they can offer in starting a business or in their career.

All women have unique strengths to empower themselves to achieve their dreams and life purpose.

Here is what one of my clients said after working with me:

"I have the confidence to break away from my present job and move towards being ME… To move forward without self-restrictions." S – QLD

This is my Y and what I love to do every day!

HELEN FROLING

Identity Empowerment Coaching

M: 0402 205 492
E: helen@identityempowerment.com.au
W: www.identityempowerment.com.au

Helen Froling is the founder of Identity Empowerment Coaching. Helen holds a degree as a Career Development Practitioner, and is an ICF accredited Professional Strengths-Based Career Counsellor and Personal Development Coach based out of the Sunshine Coast, Queensland, Australia. Helen works with her clients nationally and internationally.

A former corporate healthcare Operational Area Manager for 12 years (with an ASX Top 200 company) Helen has many years of experience in Human Resources, Business and Financial Management.

After experiencing redundancy and her own career awakening, Helen is passionate about helping introverted women to break free from unfulfilling careers, and to choose new careers more aligned with their true strengths and values. Helen works with clients showing them a less stressful and more confident method of finding their 'meant for more career and life path'.

In her spare time, you will find Helen walking her dog 'Frankie' on the beach and spending time with her husband and their two adult daughters. Some of her hobbies include photography, baking sour-dough bread, enjoying quality food with a glass of red wine or pottering around her small acreage property. Helen also loves to travel and explore unknown places; her favourite so far has been Italy, where she spent eight weeks exploring from the north to the south!

You can sign up for Helen's free newsletter (featuring tips and tools to inspire your career aspirations and life goals) or book for a free 20-minute strategy session. Sign up at her website: www.identityempowerment.com.au.

OFFER:

Your extraordinary new career and life path starts here!

Helen from Identity Empowerment Coaching is offering all Feminessence readers a A$50 discount off her coaching packages.

Use code FEMINDISC and book directly via the website www.identityempowerment.com.au

(offer expires: 1/03/2025)

Photography © Paula Brennan Photography

Activity

When you feel stuck, overwhelmed and frustrated (at work or in life) take five deep breaths and ask yourself honestly:

1. Do I have time to waste in a job that makes me unhappy?

2. Do I spend a lot of time feeling bored and unchallenged at work? Why is this?

3. Am I longing for a more purposeful career / life? How does it make me feel thinking about that?

4. If I don't make a change, what will it mean to me? How will I feel?

5. Am I ready to make a change in my career and life right now? What steps will I take to make this happen?

ANN TOMLINSON

CEO Alium Works

Rail and Construction Industry Training, Safety and Construction Management Consultant Expert

Using feminine know-how in a male-dominated industry

> *'You can let setbacks and impetuous comments define you, or you can use them to your advantage'* – AT

Ann Tomlinson is a hurdle-jumper, a barrier-breaker and a ceiling-buster. She is a visionary female entrepreneur in a male-dominated industry.

She runs a successful consulting and training business in the rail and construction industry. Wait a minute. Rail and construction? Isn't that one of the last industries in you would expect to find a female entrepreneur?

So, how did she end up in this male-dominated business?

She had always felt different. As a young child, she never felt she really fit in – and her family seemed to struggle through multiple businesses without much success, so there were few role models around to inspire her.

"At a very young age, I remember always feeling like the ugly cousin and in comparison, I was. We had a very diverse family. On the one hand you had the very successful business owners, and on the other hand you had the working-class family. That was us.

"As a child, I recall my parents starting up multiple family businesses, all of which crashed and burned. Some put it down to poor business acumen; I put it down to charity. We always had random strangers at our house who needed help. My mum was naturally attracted to what we called the 'wounded pigeon'. She was also a fixer, always trying to help someone. My dad was hard-working man and despite his effort he never really moved beyond being the brawn of the family. As a result, my empathy comes from my mum and my strong work ethic comes from my dad.

"I felt sense of not belonging. My cousins always looked pretty with their pink bows and perfect white sandals. They were very much loved by their parents and everyone in the family. Not a hair was ever out of place.

"Then there was me, and my siblings.

"As the second eldest of four children; my knees were always grazed, there were filthy hand marks all over my shirt and the occasional snot streak across my face. It was not because I liked to look like this, or because we were too poor to take a bath. I looked like this because I loved life and I was not going to be held back because I was a girl. Whatever the boys could do, I was going to do.

"Life was reasonably good. But behind a happy smile was a girl who was being sexually abused by multiple family members. For years I blamed my femininity for what had happened to me as a child. I always wonder what would have happened if I was more like a boy, more masculine, more aggressive, less submissive. Everything *wasn't* 'sugar and spice and everything nice'. We grew up in the early 80s, and at that time girls were expected to be obedient. If someone spoke, you listened. But if someone did something to you as a girl, it was because *you* didn't act like a 'proper' girl.

"I went through life rejecting who I really was. I was rejecting myself outwardly but deep inside I always knew I was destined to do great things. Finding a path back to self-acceptance would take another 30 years though!"

As you read further into Ann's story, you will come to realise the role that being female has played in her life. Although she suffered an horrific abuse of her femininity as a child, she has been able to pull herself through, and importantly, *re-discover* her feminine self as a wife, a mother and as a businesswoman.

"It was only when I became a mother to a beautiful daughter that it hit me straight between the eyes. Femininity lives inside all of us. It was always there, but because of the trauma I buried it so deep that I believed I wasn't worthy. I believed that I had to behave in a certain way to keep predators at bay.

"My now six-year-old daughter Willow is starting to experience life in a different way. She is beginning to experiment with make-up, fashion and she has become very aware of her surroundings and how people perceive her. She is a gentle and kind soul who is mature beyond her years with an EQ high enough to nurture a village.

"It wasn't until I began to experience tenderness that I knew I would have to go through a journey of self-acceptance in order to give her the best chance of success. With that, of course, comes accepting a forgiving, gentler, kinder and more loving feminine side.

"Working in rail and construction breeds a very different kind of woman. A woman who feels the need to behave in a very masculine way to be heard, to be respected and to fit in. But seeing Willow in her formative years, it became very apparent to me that this was not going to work.

"For me to influence and guide a tender young life in the right direction, I needed to tap into my own femininity. Going from a hard ass b*tch to someone who can show empathy, while still being assertive can initially be a shock to the system. But it is there. I think the hardest part for me was to accept and then trust the process. It's funny. When you go from this 'force to be reckoned with' to a softer approach, people immediately think you've lost it – or you have gone completely mad. In fact, some people reached out to me to ask if I was OK!"

How does Ann think women and men differ in the workforce, especially in the way they approach looking for a new job?

Ann feels a lot has to do with self-confidence and believing in oneself enough to be assertive, yet sensitive at the same time.

"A woman can still be assertive and influence others – but with sensitivity. Reflecting on my career and my own experience, I have allowed countless good job opportunities to slip through my hands because I felt that I was not good enough. By that I mean, 'good enough' in the sense that I did not meet 100% of the criteria. Men are the opposite. They would apply for a job with a skills match of 30% - and still feel confident that they would be shortlisted! The scary part is that they actually end up getting the job because they back themselves with an elevated ego and sense of arrogance. Research has also shown men are better at negotiating higher salaries because of their masculinity and the way they comport themselves.

"Women are more sensitive and modest, and we can be our own worst enemy at times. But I am pleased to say change is happening. The world is destined to be a better place as more people becoming aware that you can build profitable businesses, live a healthier lifestyle and create happier homes when you lead with empathy, compassion and warmth. Woman will change the world, and we see that now in world leaders like Angela Merkel, Jacinta Ardern and Kamala Harris, and our very own - Gladys Berejiklian.

"Another one of my heroines is Ruby Bridges, the American Civil Right Activist who became known to the world in 1960. Despite the adversities Ruby faced, she maintained her position in this world as the first black child to attend a white school through bravery - and by maintaining her femininity - at the tender age of six. Sure, there were other political factors at play here, but the point is, a six-year-old girl changed a powerful nation!"

Ann talks about her experiences as a mother.

"I think it's important to talk about becoming a mum. When Willow was born, there was nothing more important in my life than this little bundle of joy they placed in my arms. I was completely besotted, but little did I know I was soon to develop Post Natal Depression, which was not diagnosed for nearly six months. I didn't show signs of rejection; I was the opposite. I was completely in awe of how perfect she was. I found it difficult to accept that I was entrusted to raise a baby. You think you are ready for it - until you're not. Nobody prepares you for feeling that you've lost your identity overnight. I went from an independent woman wearing pencil skirts and stilettos to an incubator. I was running on four hours of sleep per day. I struggled and it was hard.

"To make matters worse, I was being judged. My family was standing on the sideline taking bets on how good of a mother I would turn out to be. So, when we decided to enlist the help of a nanny or registered nurse, more judgements flooded in. I could literally hear them in the popcorn stands saying 'I told you so'. It was heartbreaking to think that the people you hope would support you the most, were actually the ones breaking you down. This was a pivotal point for me.

"I am happy to say our child thrives in a social setting because we did enlist the help of others and we also sent her to early child-care. If you find the right place - which we did - your child can flourish. You can still be a good mum, wife *and* a successful businesswoman without the guilt.

"I didn't want to have to choose between being a mum and a business owner. I wanted to do both. I did - and I still do.

"We have a nanny who has been with us for most of Willow's formative years and she is exceptional. We all call her Aunty Lynn. Lynn is from the Solomon

Islands, and I could not have asked for someone better to help us raise our child. Sometimes you just have to shut out the outside noise and stop listening to what others expect you to do. Only then can you focus on doing the best that you can.

"Life wasn't handed to me on a silver platter. Everything I achieved in life is a direct response to hard work, sacrifices and sheer determination", Ann says.

She started working in the rail industry whilst living in the UK, and typically was thrown in at the deep end.

"The rail industry is very incestuous. You are either born into it, marry into it, sleep your way into it, or you know someone who can get you into it. I didn't fit into any of these categories, but because I was a 24-year-old female I was branded with the 'sleeping my way to the top' label. Despite the inaccuracy of the label, I also went through discrimination, sexual harassment, bullying and gender bias continuously for nearly six years.

"At a meeting with the Operations Manager (when I was still under the age of 25 and limited in my experience in the industry) he told me, 'If you want to play in a man's world expect to be treated the same as the guys'. My response was, 'Does that mean I will get paid the same as them?' His answer was 'No'. That conversation was the starting block of how I expected to be treated fairly and with equal opportunity.

"Sure, there were tasks that men were better at than I was, and it meant I had to work a little harder, but it never stopped me from achieving anything I set my heart on. You can let setbacks and impetuous comments define you or you can use them to your advantage. I also believe gender bias is a by-product of personal insecurity, so if someone is projecting that towards me or if they hide behind bureaucratic systems, I see it as an opportunity to surge forward. I think once you understand this, life can change for you.

"Despite working my way through the ranks and proving my worth, the reality was that I was *still* an outsider. A woman with a voice and strong will is dangerous and is treated as a troublemaker. Systems were not designed to set newcomers up for success. Companies just didn't have the framework to create a supportive work environment where new people felt safe, could ask questions, or connect with mentors. It was a sink or swim situation.

"Fast forward to more recent years, I realised that little has changed. When I oversaw multi-million-dollar projects here in Australia, I made sure my team members were treated fairly and with respect, and that everyone was on an equal pay scale. I knew more had to be done in this space. I wanted to make an impact on a much larger scale and oddly enough there was this huge void in the market, which was completely untapped.

"That's why I established Alium Works in 2018. I wanted to create a level playing for *all* job seekers in Australia. I had seen too many applicants be rejected because they didn't have the perfect exam scores; they were considered too this or too that. I wanted to create a platform where I could cut through the bureaucratic recruitment systems and showcase people for *who* they are as opposed to just having a polished resume.

"My defining moment was when I decided to expand my business model to become a Registered Training Organisation in 2020. For years I listened to industry experts (all males!) who said I wasn't ready, there was too much compliance, it was too much this and too much that, and I couldn't achieve it in the timeframes I suggested. Some even said that I was too inexperienced and too young, even though I have worked in compliance roles for over 18 years, and I turned 40 last year!

"I listened to this for nearly two years until an unrelated opportunity presented itself last year and I decided to listen to my intuition, silence the self-doubt and stop believing the so-called experts. Once I made the decision to become an RTO and move forward, everyone jumped on the bandwagon and helped me make it happen. With the support of my husband and a young team we prepared an application in less than three months and waited another three months for the outcome. I am pleased to say we became a Registered Training Organisation on 5 January 2021!

"Taking a few steps back, the defining point was when I made the call to my business coach and told her what I wanted to do and how I proposed to do it. Her response was brief and to the point. She said, 'What took you so long?'

"What was perplexing and confronting about this was that I allowed industry experts to influence my decision-making process. I always thought I was in control. But the opposite was true. It wasn't until a complete outsider to the industry pointed out a few home truths that the penny dropped for me. I believe that up until that moment I was institutionalised.

"When making business decisions, I now consult with *female leaders* outside of our industry. They bring fresh perspective and, as a result, new business growth.

"Drawing from my own challenges as a female, I knew there were better ways of attracting better quality candidates, irrespective of their gender and cultural background. Due to the success of the programs we offer, we are now heavily involved in creating pathways in Rail and Construction. We are also working with High Schools to educate young woman about opportunities in these sectors.

"I've had friends say their daughter wants to be like me. It is very flattering, but besides being a boost to my echo it is inspiring to hear that through the work I do, other women - especially young women - can see that it is possible to be a mother, to be an individual, a wife and successful businesswoman *without* having to sacrifice one's femininity. You can still be strong, while being tender. You can still be assertive and show compassion.

"One of the members in our community (Liz) came to us when she was just about ready to give up on life. The life had literally been sucked out of her. After years working in child-care, she could not see a way out. After working with me and some of our other mentors, she has completely turned her life around. Liz has found her purpose in life again. She is now actively applying for roles that will help her progress to get the life and lifestyle she so deserves."

Ann has learnt how to connect with her own femininity and uses it as a way to *strengthen* her skills and abilities in the business world.

"There are now more females in high profile leadership roles in the rail and construction business. They are exceptionally good at what they do, but what sets them apart is their ability to influence and I believe that comes from *showing femininity*. You don't have to rule with an iron fist to get things done. **You attract more butterflies by planting flowers, not by casting a net!**

"Women are exceptional at creating more opportunities for other women. So, my advice would be to ignore the stereotypical banter that you must behave in a certain way.

"People want to meet the real you, so be authentic and be true to your own personal brand."

ANN TOMLINSON

Founder and Director, Alium Works

M: 0427 285 775
E: ann@aliumworks.com.au
W: www.aliumworks.com.au/about

As the founder and director of Alium Works, Ann Tomlinson works with job seekers and employers in the rail and construction industries. Alium Works' primary aim is to increase capability for more productive, rewarding and safer workplaces.

Ann has over 20 years of experience working in the traditionally male-dominated rail industry, including holding senior roles leading multi-million-dollar projects in Australia and internationally. She is passionate about providing rewarding careers to motivated job seekers from a wide range of backgrounds, and uses cutting edge technology that has employers embracing new ways to find and develop future leaders.

Ann has been recognised both personally and professionally for her commitment to innovation and creating pathways with an AusMumpreneur 'Women will Change the World Award' in 2020, a Digital Transformation Award in 2020 and a Diversity Award in 2019 for her career-building Pathway Program.

With her signature warm, no B.S. approach and constant focus on continuous improvement, Ann is leading the charge with new ways to improve people outcomes in rail and construction. Her focus is on providing opportunities and pathways for career growth to a broad range of job seekers, while she uses ground-breaking technology to help leading employers to acquire, grow and retain the right talent.

Photography © Images by Zahrina Robertson Photography and Video

Activity

My story has been about learning to balance masculine and feminine energies to succeed in a traditionally male dominated industry, while I raise my daughter.

From my own experience and observation, I see successful women getting caught up using masculine energy to try and create 'a level playing field', and that can be counterproductive.

1. Think about how you've succeeded in your career or business. Have you used mainly masculine or feminine energy ... or both? If needed, how can you balance these energies?

____

____

____

2. What would you say to a younger you about successfully balancing masculine and feminine energy?

____

____

____

3. If you're a parent (or carer, auntie, grandma, godparent, mentor), how do you want to show up for the kids in your life with balancing masculine and feminine energy?

____

____

____

4. When it comes to balancing masculine and feminine energy to build a career or business, how can you be an effective role model for young people?

____

____

____

154

UNLOCK YOUR FEMINESSENCE® CODE

SAVANNAH FALZON

Retirement Care Specialist

Personalised, ethical and respectful elder care

Just like the Phoenix I rose from the ashes, the strength within to rise again, more beautiful and courageous than ever before' – SF

I was born in Sydney to two loving parents, who had migrated from across the world, from a small island in the Mediterranean called Malta.

My parents met in Australia after they realised that they had little future and job prospects in their home country. They were introduced to each other by the local priest and after 12 months of dating, married in 1967. I was conceived after 18 months and became Dad's 'little princess'. Being the eldest and a girl came with a lot of expectations and a great deal of confusion on my part. I enjoyed playing outdoors and even though I was a bit of a tomboy, (this was frowned upon particularly by Mum) I always needed to present myself at my best, by dressing appropriately. Even as an adult and married woman, Mum would suggest I put on a bit of make-up and look pretty, especially when my husband came home. To the day she passed away, we would have our discussions over wearing 'lippy.'

As a young child I remember wanting to be independent and to choose my own clothes. I suppose I was searching for my identity. At the age of five we travelled to Malta for six months to visit family. One particular incident that remains a strong memory in my life involves my grandmother. We were getting ready to go on a family outing and I was selecting my outfit (as I normally would), however this day my grandmother put a stop to my being allowed to choose my own clothes. She was clearly angry with both Mum and me. She told my mother that I should not be allowed to decide what to wear. She felt this could lead to me 'trying to control' my mother, and what I did. My ability to have some sense of control over parts of my life changed in so many ways from that day.

I have a brother just three years younger, yet the difference in what was expected from us, (between the sexes) was huge in our family. My Dad was a very hands-on father, taking us to sporting events, getting us ready for school, making lunches, cleaning and ironing uniforms and polishing our shoes. Dad even did the weekly shop. In our family Mum would cook and Dad would clean up; I did not know any different. Mum, worked very hard. She worked 6 days a week early starts, long days to contribute to the family to enable us to live a comfortable life. My parents worked together to achieve their goal of the Australian dream to own their home. This was to be a huge shock in years to come, because whilst married those expectations were clearly not met and they caused many problems between my husband and myself. We didn't share the same goals and dreams as a couple.

While we were young, it was my responsibility to take my brother to school and bring him home safely - that was when we were just eight and five years of age. As we grew older, the expectations started to shift, and it was understood that he should now look after me - as he was a boy and both taller and stronger than I was.

As an Australian born girl with Maltese heritage, I was expected to follow my parents' traditions; to do as they said and not be heard; to be a well-behaved girl, respect my elders and not cause them any embarrassment. I had a strict upbringing in which we attended Church regularly. In hindsight, I obeyed their rules to the detriment of my personal growth. In my eyes I was always the good girl, following the rules and 'staying between the lines'. But I felt I was never good enough, particularly in my Mum's eyes.

In my late teens, I struggled to get my parents to understand my need for independence, to carve out my own identity and to lead my life on my terms. I felt trapped living at home. My parents refused to let me travel overseas with my fiancé at the age of 21 so, in an attempt to live my life my way, I married him the following year. In hindsight, I was not equipped with the maturity or the required life skills at such a young age. My expectations for myself as a daughter, wife and mother were based on a false reality and the need to seek constant approval.

I have had several setbacks in terms of connecting to my best feminine self, many coming from within; a lack of confidence and low self-esteem in the past has inhibited my growth and potential.

I married far too young, of course very much in love, yet naïve regarding the role of wife and mother. I remember ringing Dad to ask how to use the washing machine. I really only had my parents' marriage to guide me, and at the time I thought they had a pretty good marriage. My ex-husband and I did not see eye to eye on numerous things, particularly how we raised our children. He felt I did too much for our family. We were from different cultures, which I believe contributed to the breakdown of our marriage.

I gave birth to my first child in 1994, it was trying to live up to the high expectations of others that led me to being diagnosed with postnatal depression. It took time to realise I had nothing to prove to anyone. I was the one self-sabotaging myself, my dreams and my relationships. I needed to rebuild my relationship with myself first and too truly love myself unconditionally in order to receive unconditional love in return.

Our separation and divorce took place in 2003, sending me on a roller coaster journey for the next 17 years, with many highs and lows. My self-esteem and self-confidence were left destroyed and were to continue to contribute to more setbacks, disappointments and problems, which resulted in poor choices for myself and my children. Unfortunately, I met my second husband on the rebound, only eight months after the split. It was my second marriage that saw me fall to the lowest times in my life, as he turned out to be an alcoholic with a toxic personality. After seven years of marriage (with three separations during that period), my children and I were delivered a final blow when we had to seek a Domestic Violence Order in order to protect ourselves. It was the most harrowing and frightening thing I have ever had to do in my life.

After all the drama and three years of living in fear, my lightbulb moment occurred. I was no longer the victim; I was the survivor. I found the lioness within me, and my feminine power to live life to the fullest. I chose to no longer live in shame with regards to my past. It may be part of my story (that I cannot deny), however, it does not define me nor inhibit me from soaring to great heights.

When I became a single mum (as my ex-husband moved away in 2005), my work life completely revolved around my family life. I only accepted positions that suited my children and parents (as they were ageing and needed care).

Since then, my children are independent adults living their own lives and dreams, and I now have the freedom to focus on my own personal growth and the growth of my business.

Over time I healed. I forgave myself first and then forgave others. It took time and years of internal work through counselling, attending retreats, and various learnt techniques (such as tapping) to become the person I love today. I finally found the inner peace I was searching for and now I live my life with purpose - the way I was naturally born to live - with my feminine power shining brightly.

When my mother passed away in 2019, I think I went through a transformation and rebirth of who I really am. I had been playing it small in my business and had lived in fear of judgement, from myself and from my Mum, whenever I needed to make decisions. I was always made to feel I gave too much, but it was never enough for Mum. I was in constant inner turmoil, juggling my energies with so many people.

During this period of renewal and growth in 2019 I met the most amazing man; my life partner who loves me unconditionally and understands the demands of my life, my family, and my business. We manage life together; it's no longer a juggling act, it's a way of life for us. This is the first time I have been given the support to live my life naturally, in my feminine power.

Prior to mum passing away, I juggled caring for her and starting my business. Keeping things small enabled me to provide a quality service to a small number of clients, and meant I was able to be there for Mum whenever she needed me.

Since Mum's passing, my feminine side, which is intuitively nurturing, empathetic, passionate, and compassionate has flourished - I continue to love and give. These values and qualities have helped me to develop my business further in the past two years, and they have given me the strength to grow my company and continue to have the foresight to develop new services. It is my feminine side that enables me to make a difference in the lives of my family, friends and clients, which for me now comes naturally.

I have three amazing children who are everything to me. I had my first child at the age of 25, at a time when my career in public service was on the rise. I was one of the youngest managers in our Department, but as I chose my family over my career. It was while juggling motherhood and work life that I decided to take a step back from management and went in a different direction into Policy Management (rather than front line management) – this was to reduce the stress on my family. Placing my daughter in family day care was one of the hardest decisions, and I remember driving away in tears, wondering how I could leave her with a stranger when she was just eight months old. When she was two and a half years old (I was pregnant with my second child), an opportunity to move to Queensland came up. We decided this would enable me to stay at home and raise our children without the stresses of juggling my personal life and work.

I continued to stay at home until my third child was 18 months. It was around this time that I began to feel lost and without my own identity. I felt I was just a wife, mother and daughter but 'Who was I really?' I began my journey of learning and enrolled in an online University course - which I thoroughly enjoyed.

I later went on to study Remedial Massage and Naturopathy but was unable to complete this course for financial reasons and due to a change in circumstances, which required me to put family first. However, later in life I went onto to study and completed my Real Estate Certificate, which has allowed me (over the past 10 years) to become a full-time Real Estate Agent. More recently this has helped compliment my business offering with the additional of a Real Estate consultancy services for elderly clients in need of assistance when selling their home.

My essence as a woman involves my feminine power: to live with grace, beauty, warmth, empathy and humility. As I have matured and nurtured my feminine power 'my being' has grown, become enhanced and blossomed. I have learnt there is power in silence, as it is through my silence that my inner voice and intuition have flourished. This is where I gain my inner strength. Where once I was made to feel that I was too sensitive, too emotional, too affectionate I now know this is my feminine power and I embrace it. It is who I am.

I am feminine, and I love all of me.

And how do I think women contribute effectively in a business world run mostly by men? Women see the world in grey, not just black and white. I believe with my nurturing and compassionate feminine side, I can also display characteristics of strength, resilience, courage, and independence. These values and qualities have helped me to develop my business, given me the strength to grow the business and continue to have the foresight to develop new services. It is my feminine side that enables me to make a difference in the lives of my clients, which for me as a woman comes naturally and ultimately has contributed to my success.

Many women hold themselves back from success. For many, it is not the fear of failure but rather the fear of success; it is self-sabotage; it's a woman's upbringing and self-limiting beliefs, asking themselves "What makes you so special to think you can be successful?" It can be a lack of support from family and friends. For me, it was finally admitting that it was *me that held me* back and it was not until I believed I was truly successful in all facets of my personal life, my family life and my business that I began to soar to greater heights.

My business, Retirement Care Solutions (RCS) is a unique boutique consultancy that commenced trading in late 2015. For the past five years, my business has provided comprehensive downsizing, retirement care and aged care support solutions for ageing consumers and their families in South East Queensland and even interstate.

The business concept grew from my own experiences with my ageing mother and from my work as a Real Estate Agent. When my father passed away in 2008 (from a long battle with prostate cancer), Mum's life and mine changed forever. Mum's world revolved around caring for him and providing support as his wife, but after he died she did not know what to do with herself. Her decline became noticeable and it was worrying too me. Within 12 months of his death, I assisted Mum with the sale of her home and moved her to a retirement village. It was this experience (together with our lack of knowledge of the options available to us) that made me realise we could have done things differently - and with a better outcome.

In my work as a Real Estate Agent, I recognised and regularly witnessed the confusion and distress experienced by older people needing to downsize and sell. It was seeing how difficult it was for family members transitioning an elderly loved one into care that led me to create this business.

Prior to launching Retirement Care Solutions, I worked in the retirement industry for over two years, and it was because of this experience I recognised that retirement and aged care living was not a 'one-shoe fits-all' approach. My intention in creating this business was to ease the stress and help simplify the minefield of choices, options and decisions, which clients and their families face. I established a service focused on providing practical and informative support for individuals transitioning from owner-occupied to retirement village or aged care living.

Today, my team of committed contractors and I are passionate about helping clients overcome the confusion or fear they feel in taking that next step in their ageing journey. We offer a service that is affordable, compassionate and client-centric. We take away the hassle and gives retirees, older seniors and their families peace of mind - knowing they have made the best decision for themselves or their loved ones. As an independently owned and operated service, we take no referral fees or commission from retirement living or aged care providers. This means that our team can take pride in offering unbiased, tailored and holistic services that keep our client's best interests, needs and wishes at the absolute centre of all decision-making.

Our services have provided us with many heart-warming and successful happy endings for our clients. We often see our clients and their loved ones at their worst, many coming to us in crisis situations, in hospital and not allowed to return home. We come into their lives to restore hope, and to provide solutions to enable our clients to live their remaining months or years with dignity and respect.

One of our success stories is of an elderly lady aged 86, a widow of many years and a mother of nine children. She was living a lonely existence in her home. She was comfortable, however, due to illness and mobility problems, her ability to leave her home independently was limited; added to this was the fact that her family lived about an hour away, so family visits were also limited. I came into her life when she decided this was not how she wanted to continue living. We explored the options available to her, and I recommended trying respite care for a period of two weeks to see how she would adapt.

Her son and daughter in law attended the inspections and after looking at three facilities they decided on the particular one they liked, as it ticked the boxes. The time came to start her respite period, but within two days I received a phone call from her asking if she could stay. She did not want to go home; she had found her new home and was enjoying the activities, and the company of other residents and staff. For the first time in her life she had her nails painted! This still brings a smile to my face and fills me with joy. This is why I do what I do. I want to ensure I can change our loved one's lives for the better, that our solutions improve our client's lives.

My work gives me immense satisfaction. And with it comes a feeling that I can truly say I finally love myself, accept myself and continue to empower myself to achieve all that life has to offer. In return, I now have the most loving relationships with my partner, children, family and friends.

Life has come full circle. And it's about love, joy and contentment.

SAVANNAH FALZON

Retirement Care Solutions

M: 0408 451 667
E: savannah@retirementcaresolutions.com.au
W: www.retirementcaresolutions.com.au

I am Savannah Falzon, a mum of three, a sister, a partner, an aunty, a friend and business owner. I have worked in the Retirement and Aged Care industry for over seven years, and established Retirement Care Solutions.

Retirement Care Solutions is Your One Stop Retirement Shop. I am passionate about assisting retirees to enjoy their retirement years and supporting our elderly to live their last years in an enjoyable and safe environment - whether that is helping them remain in their own home or transition to Residential Care. We assist retirees and their families by helping to facilitate their move (from home to Residential Care), so it is smooth and easy. This process is often described as a 'minefield', where many individuals are too afraid to step into the unknown for fear of getting it wrong, not knowing where to start or where it will all end. I provide solutions and assist my clients every step of the way, ensuring their needs are in safe hands.

We address each aspect of the process with our clients - from the door-to-door service of visiting the communities and facilities with clients and/or loved ones, to assisting with decluttering and preparing their home for sale and then selling it, to redirecting and connecting utilities and services in their new home. We even assist and complete the paperwork for Centrelink. We are able to give our clients the peace of mind they are looking for as we are there to help them through their journey from start to finish.

I envision Retirement Care Solutions will continue to grow from strength to strength, providing our services across all of Australia. I want Retirement Care Solutions to be the first choice for retirees and seniors when they are considering a move into Retirement Living and Aged Care.

OFFER:

For Feminessence® readers I would like to offer a 1-hour complimentary Analysis and Consultation and 10% off Fixed Fee Packages booked mentioning Feminessence®.

Photography © Annie Noon Fotoforce Photography

Activity

Take a moment to answer the following questions. Jot down any notes and questions that come to mind as you consider each question, and determine what you need to take action on.

1. Is your loved ones Estate Planning in order?

____

____

____

2. If a crisis was to occur in your loved ones life are you both prepared?

____

____

____

3. If not, do you know where to begin?

____

____

____

4. What types of care have you considered for your loved ones?

____

____

____

5. Do you know what to consider when looking for Residential Care for your loved ones?

____

____

____

From homeless to millionaire

> 'Out of adversity, anything is possible' – ES

My name is Elissa Scott and I'm 53 years old. Growing up, my parent's expectations were very negative. My life was full of emotional and physical pain. A child should not have to experience what I saw in life. I grew up in a loveless family, one full of destruction, and verbal and emotional abuse. I was never praised; just put down, called names and tortured. It was hell on earth.

My expectations were that of a failure.

This built me up to become the strongest soul on the planet. It was a blessing, because without those 17 years of abuse I would not have done nor achieved the life that I created for myself. It's very hard on the mind to live with a narcissistic 'Dr Jekyll/Mr Hyde' type personality. I knew I was going to change the cycle and never ever, ever bring my child or children up in a family circle of hatred, sadness and pure evil. I still to this day believe alcohol is the root of all evil.

Being bullied at school didn't help either and I had no friends. It was a very hard time. I was so lonely. I would go to school, attend roll call and then leave - off to the station to travel the trains looking for adventure, to be loved, or a loving family home I could attach too.

When I was locked out of the house I would lie outside on the grass for hours. I would look at the clouds and their shapes, and bawl my eyes out. Sometimes the clouds would make nice happy shapes and it made me smile. One particular day, I remember looking at this tree when I was locked in my bedroom. It swayed in the wind and I asked it to send me someone to love me for me, all of me - so one day I could be free. I suppose this was the first day I realised my special connection to the universe and nature.

I had to learn from all the negative comments I received. I learnt from them what my responses should be. I learnt that being teased, called nasty names, being unwanted, unpopular, laughed at, continuously bullied and hit, would be my preparation for my future - as hard and sad as it was to be.

After running away and escaping one morning, my mother yelled after me that if I left, I could never come back. I was ok with that. I was strong as I marched up the street. I remember looking down the road and no-one came after me. No-one ever came. Hours later, I called home to be yelled at and I said I would only return if I was not hit. I went back but nothing ever changed. It was a nightmare, day in and day out.

Do you know what it's like to be belted, hit, slapped and punched in your face, across your bare little legs, straight onto your arms and around your head? Do you know what it's like to be locked outside; not even allowed to go to the toilet and having 'to go' in the bush, while your dad is inside with women partying, drinking and making sure you were nowhere to be found?

I confronted him throughout the years; it just fell on deaf ears. His denial was his way of dealing with the horror stories of his behaviour, while fuelled with alcohol.

I had to overcome a constant torrent of harsh words and abuse that I wasn't good enough, that I was unlovable, and ugly, a failure and that everyone hated me. It was a really bad place to be in, but it was what it was. **After my three suicide attempts failed, I chose to live.**

When I was 17, I had a friend who was a Maths teacher at my school. He understood how I was feeling and was 'a light in a dark tunnel'. But he ended his life after I left the school. I also had another Maths teacher at another school when I was 16; her husband was my friend, he raped me one lunch time. She then remarried and her new husband made sure we didn't connect again. She passed away from Breast Cancer last year.

Throughout it ALL, I always knew someone else was worse off than me.

After living in London for four years after school, I returned to Australia and started a job at the local Real Estate agency in office/sales administration. I had made up my mind to leave after a year-and-a-half to travel around Australia and back overseas for a friend's wedding, but I never went. Instead, I started a relationship with the boss, Michael (who had three daughters). We ran away and eloped. I became a stepmother to three little girls - Carla, Lauren and Kimberley, and three years later, we had James.

But we were so poor. Michael lost everything in his divorce from his first wife; we had no home, just love and a tent.

I have so many wonderful, fond and funny memories with my three little mates, and experienced love, life and happiness for the first time in my life. What a journey! I have no regrets. For the next 22 years I grew up in the marriage and so did the girls, following their paths to motherhood, marriage and boyfriends. Marrying their father, who was 13 years older (a father figure) gave me the family security I always wanted and needed. We stuck it out for 22 years of marriage and we were together for two years before our marriage. I became a stepmother at the age of 23; Carla was seven, Lauren was four and Kimberley was two years old. We were a unit for three years until James (my son) came along. Michael was the 'love' of my life. It is nice to be able to call him my friend still, to this day. Helen, Michael's first wife is also my good friend and now a mighty fine grandmother!

You do play second fiddle to your family when it is a mixed family - but we were a team. It was never 'you, me and them'. The best decision I ever made was to become friends with Michael's daughters, for all of us to be team members, because they already had their own mother (Helen - a great cook). Being friends with your stepchildren is what I think leads to a perfect relationship. We were in this together. They are champion little ladies, and I love them to bits!

We discovered our femininity together. It is a beautiful puzzle joined together through each stage of their lives; the ups, the downs and more laughter than tears. They were my mates, and we did everything together. When we were so poor, we took our dented car with three hubcaps (while listening to a Rod Stewart cassette) around to people's rubbish tips and collected all the treasure. Then we had our own little garage sales. Before this we all lived in a tent, then upgraded to a caravan, then the mobile home and finally our own home.

Being a stepmother, a mother to my own son and having a husband on commission type wages was such hard work. I had three jobs before I had James and worked up to the day before delivery. Then, because he was a sick little boy, I had to put him into care after a month of being home. And the ultimate test of my female power? It was when I had to turn the machines off on my newborn son James while in intensive care. I was told he would either live or die! OMG... Then to be told I needed a shot of Anti D in case he died - no one could tell me if it had to be tested for HIV/Aids! Hectic times!

I went from one job to another, always searching for what it was that I was meant to do. Eventually I owned and operated my own recruitment company and retired at the age of 40.

It is so important to be true to yourself, walk your truth, and live to the beat of your own drum. Life is short. Life owes you nothing, so go make your own life and don't be a victim to your circumstances. Challenge yourself to waltz through doors to see what is on the other side. It doesn't really matter what happens as long as you give it a go. My husband helped me understand I needed to love **myself.** I needed to grow old naturally and to be happy in my own skin, but it is not easy when your whole life you have been told differently.

I am a very lucky lady, but I create my luck. Why not decide today that 'No' means 'Yes'? Lol such fun!

I've decided I want to live to 84 years old and as I'm dying I will mutter the words 'What a ride!!!...' and 'Absolutely NO REGRETS'. So many people wish their lives away, but I ***action*** my life and that is the difference.

You will never know unless you give it a go. Take that first step, I dareeeeee you...

Many humans only exist, never really living to their true full potential.

As they say: Out of adversity anything truly is possible.

Living naturally and 'being real' (on my journey across Earth) has created such a beautiful path as I weave in and out of doors all over the world - just to see what I can find.

We aren't here for a long time, just a fun time.

The essence of femininity for me is that one can be identified as a BIG lotus flower, stuck in the mud, but with the most amazing acceptance for oneself at the cost of all that is lost. You can shine and rise above all to forgive and conquer. You can create magic out of pure loneliness, adversity, manipulation and control, and you can strive for what you want. You just have to believe; believe from your mind, heart and soul. Believe there is always someone else out there who has had it tougher. The beauty in my journey is forgiveness; really, I can connect, inspire and love women all over the world after the mean horrible things they did to me for years and years throughout my life.

My life was not always easy, and it is really interesting that in spite of being bullied and hated by women for so many years, I can now serve, communicate and love so many women with my tea. I think giving up alcohol was also a major turning point in my life - allowing me to reclaim my true self. Once I knew I was going to be ok; I began to shine.

I have a very strong business sense and when you are stripped back to the raw bone, you have no choice but to pick yourself up, focus, plan, think, share and go for it.

So, how and why did I launch **The T Lady's - Menopause Tea?** As I personally approached my next stage in life, I wanted to look into natural alternatives for the relief of menopause symptoms.

I didn't know too much about Menopause, so my mission started with research. My intention was to create and to bring to life a certified organic caffeine free natural tea for women worldwide.

Menopause Tea Hot Flush Tea has signed contracts (thanks to Mark Smith, Bruno Disotto, Kruno Konyit, John O'Kelly and Helen Maxwell) with IGA supermarkets, FoodWorks, Ritchies IGA's, Foodland supermarkets and various independent cafes and shops. I would also like to thank Kathryn Powell and Michelle Besant from Complete Health Products (QLD distributors). We are independent, community focused and charitable companies - a perfect fit for my soul. We support Australian jobs and Menopause Tea is a proud supporter of Ovarian Cancer Australia (one in four women die from Ovarian Cancer). I think it is important to have an ethical and honest approach in business. It's a community affair - (my tea packers/telemarketers have been the homeless, survivors of domestic violence or have had struggles with mental health issues). We are a team - not them but 'us'.

My clients range from those in their teenage years to 94-year-olds. Menopausal women have told me they have put their teenage daughters on my tea (for period cramps) and the elderly have called to let me know they are sleeping better in nursing homes (after buying my tea on bus trips). We have developed trial packs, subscriptions and monthly packs available for purchase online.

My goal is to let every single person in the whole world know that I have a tea bag for Menopause and its different stages. Even if a stranger on the street asks me for directions, I have made it my mission to pop the old tea bag promotion into the conversation. It is such fun!

I launched **Menopause Tea** with my own savings. I had no business loan, no family loans or support, just my hard-earned dollars. I am just a girl with a dream who wants to leave footprints in the Earth, that's me! I want to leave a legacy for humankind, one that supports women's health, saves marriages, and can supply and support women with a natural alternative in a chemically driven world.

What motivates me is to see dreams come true, make life fun; know the universe will deliver what you want, you just have to ask. I'm living proof.

My success has been recorded by the number of women who contact me from all around the world - whether to enquire about the tea or send in a testimonial. Selling one tea bag is pure success to me. For the rest of my life I will enjoy the Menopause tea stories, its journey around the globe - as we all know tea loves to travel!

I believe the key to success is to be happy. Happy in your own skin. Be thankful and grateful. When you ask lots of questions you have power and I believe knowledge is power. Everyone loves to talk about themselves; it's really interesting to watch. So, watch carefully you can even get answers to your own thoughts and questions from and by others.

Back in 2016, I remember calling the tea-making man (Kym Grant) and being told the minimum order was 10,000 tea bags, which I could not afford at the time. We agreed on 2,000, but even then, I was wondering how on earth was I going to sell 2,000 tea bags! We have now sold over 300,000 tea bags in the market. How cool is that?

What do I think is the essence of Femininity?

To me, it is about identifying your natural instincts and understanding that you have a gift to tap into and share with the world. It is about being real, truthful and honest with all your dealings in your personal and business life.

Own your matter, whether you have made mistakes or not and walk your truth.

Always be a candle in your life - shine and burn bright.

When we truly honour each other as humans and embrace the beauty within one another we are expressing our Feminessence®. I am always so excited to hear when someone I know, or a complete stranger has done well. Why do we continuously look and live like our neighbours at the detriment of our **own** soul and **its** journey? We all have our own unique fingerprints; we are all one of a kind. You have to own your inner beauty and gifts. We all have them. Seek and you will find. Once you do, it is so powerful. What is your gift to the world?

So why not add a charity to my **already full-time life?** 'Homeless No More' is my charity, which I launched back in 2011 with two other ladies.

Homeless No More has a 100 percent success rate of housing the homeless with no government funding. We reconnect families and assist people with launching their own businesses or gaining employment. The homeless love/ loved me unconditionally. I found my home. I have met the most amazing people out on the streets and in the Developing World. By paying forward and random acts of kindness, we have become the heartbeat of the community and together we have achieved amazing results and statistics.

Under our charity umbrella we have launched the 'Suicide Prevention Care Boxes' for men and women (made by the various Men's Sheds and distributed through Lifeline and Beyond Blue), the 'Leave 4 Good Escape Boxes' (for domestic violence victims) and the 'Save our Farmers Campaign' with Kim Bunting (for individuals recovering from droughts and bushfires).

I have worked on my own social enterprises in Papua New Guinea; building houses and teaching local women how to make profit out of natural resources. I also worked in Madagascar with the poorest people on the planet; launching businesses, teaching, promoting natural resources for profit and volunteering in remote areas, along with building local homes. Truly, out of poverty, entrepreneurs are born.

The rest of my days are filled with paying forward and random acts of kindness all over the world.

I launched five interactive recruitment business units in the global financial crisis, plus I opened a home-based facial business and palm-reading service, created designs for Menopausal soaps/sprays/bath-bombs/creams (testing these in the market before COVID-19) and ended up buying 32 acres in regional Australia with my toy boy and best friend Brett. We are now proud owners of two dogs, four goats and one chook!

There are a million reasons to smile! Work/life balance? Create this for yourself. It's your choice, seriously.

How lucky is it to wake every day and do what you want? Being in control of your destiny. I am living a simple, minimalistic happily ever after; never to the beat of anyone else's drum ever again. Some of you may think that living in posh areas and owning three cars, working many many hours, stressing about mortgage repayments, and changing your faces and lips to look like someone else will make you happy, but in my reflection it won't. I, for one, will be off somewhere searching for my next adventure! Growing old gracefully, a recluse, just how nature intended it to be!

We all have choices. Remember every single decision you make creates your destiny. We all have one set of individual fingerprints, so make them your own. Together, we can do this. I believe in the power of 'Thank you'. No one really says thank you these days, but if you do, it will always be remembered.

It only takes a second to change. It's your choice.

A final point about COVID-19. What a wonderful thing for the Earth! Not the deaths of course, but to reconnect one human to another. I can't wait for the brand-new world! You know this is strange but accidently I got to speak to my dad again after all these years apart. I got to thank him for being the biggest jerk on the planet because without the pain, torture, emotional, physical and mental abuse I would not be where I am today, sharing love, fun, laughter and adventure with everyone I meet. Life is short. So what are you doing today to make someone else's life just that little bit better?

Kindness rocks...

'The beauty in my journey is forgiveness' – ES

ELISSA SCOTT

The T Lady

M: 0403 139 603
E: menopauset@gmail.com
W: www.menopauset.com

What a ride Elissa Scott has been on; she can't believe she made it!

Elissa endured 17 years of family domestic violence, during which she was physically, mentally and emotionally abused. She was also badly bullied during school.

After escaping to the UK, working and travelling whenever and with whomever, Elissa returned to Australia broken hearted. Pulling herself together she started her career in Real Estate.

Marrying the boss was easy, becoming a stepmother to three little girls interesting and a mum to son James divine.

1999 - Elissa launched her own recruitment company/recruitment workshops - retiring at 40 years old, debt free.

2011 - Elissa launched Homeless No More - a charity impacting lives within Australia and worldwide. Specialising in homelessness, social enterprises in the Developing World, suicide prevention, domestic violence, and drought and fire initiatives for struggling farmers.

2013 - Elissa and her stepdaughter Carla walked the Kokoda Track supporting Wayside Chapel Kings Cross.

2014 - Elissa launched Kokoda Roots Adventures in Papua New Guinea, a tour group which supports education, housing and employment for local communities.

2015 - Elissa participated in building works, social enterprises in business and taught English and hygiene classes in Madagascar.

2016 - Elissa created The T Lady - Menopause Tea Hot Flush Tea, a certified organic caffeine free herbal tea for menopausal women worldwide, supporting Ovarian Cancer Australia. You will often hear out on the streets, that the tea packers in her business have been given chances of employment - having suffered from mental health issues, homelessness or domestic violence.

This woman is truly remarkable. Enjoy her story!

OFFER:

Menopause Tea - Hot Flush Tea

Buy one get one free offer expires 4 November 2021

Activity

You only have one life to live. You know deep in your soul that time is of the essence.

Can you please stop (just for a second, just stop, stand still) and self-talk this question out with your SOUL? Out loud ask yourself: 'What is actually holding me back?' Be totally honest.

I know I want to live to my true potential and not just exist in this lifetime. If you can hold your dreams loosely in your mind (breathe and listen to your heart and it's beat) ask yourself: 'Will I ever get to MY start line?', 'Can today be MY day?' So, go on grab your shadow and go for it. Why Not?

Don't dream your life, action your life!

Ask yourself seriously: 'What have I done today to move my business venture or dreams forward?'

Let's talk about FEAR! FEAR - a four letter word that holds so much POWER. Fear of failure, fear of success - is that what you're thinking? Let's do this exercise together: grab a piece of paper, please write the word down FEAR in blue or black pen. Look at the word, say it both in your mind and then out loud... now burn it. See there's nothing to worry about, it's gone in a second - out of mind, out of sight! Too true!

Decisions = Destiny! Choose wisely!

SAMANTHA RICHARDS

CEO/Founder, Building Voices Public Speaking

Teaching the art of confident communication

> '*Every single woman on this planet deserves to have a voice and be heard*' – SR

How many of us are terrified of speaking in front of a crowd? We become tongue-tied and anxious; we worry about being judged; we lose our confidence and self-esteem. Frankly, we wish we could just disappear off the face of the earth!

Samantha Richards understands your fears. Her business, **Building Voices Public Speaking**, has helped numerous children to speak confidently in front of their classmates, and helped adults to enrich both their business and personal lives by teaching them how to communicate effectively, (without panicking) in any situation. It is a skill that everyone needs to master.

Samantha is not Australian by birth – and her early life was by no means easy.

This might surprise you, seeing how masterfully she understands the art of communicating with others, so that they can promote themselves and their brand to become successful business leaders.

"At the age of four-and-a-half, my family moved from the UK to Iran, where we lived until 1978. I was nine when the revolution that toppled the reign of the last Shah took place, and we were evacuated with nothing but the clothes on our backs. We returned to the UK, where I had to adapt to a new way of life.

"Although I could speak English fluently, I could neither read nor write the language proficiently, so achieving English literacy was my first hurdle. I was placed into a school where I was publicly ridiculed for my illiteracy. I was the ten-year-old kid whose teacher repeatedly told me I was stupid and would amount to nothing in life. Sadly, I believed her, and those cruel words buried themselves in my heart for three decades. I stopped trying academically, *'if she thinks I'm stupid, then I must be,'* my 10-year-old mind reasoned. I stopped believing in myself.

"I then moved to Africa, and for ten years lived through much more than the average child of my age. At the age of 14, I moved to Nigeria from Sudan, where I put intravenous drips into newborn babies (to help save their lives) at the local hospital in Shaki. It was also in Shaki where I witnessed a ritualistic killing of a girl.

"I always loved being outside, exploring each place I lived in and would often walk a long way from home as I investigated different areas of the village.

"That day, I had heard an ear-piercing scream. I followed the sound, eventually peering through a crack in the door of a hut. A man was chanting, and there was a strange burning of herbs. I saw a girl lying on a makeshift altar. She looked to be around my age, maybe a little younger. She was unconscious. I was about to rush in and help her, but I became rooted to the spot in terror when I saw the dagger.

"I didn't know what was happening. My instinct has always been to help others in need - which was why I had followed the noise. As I stood there in horror watching the girl die, I heard a voice in my head shout, 'IF YOU CAN SEE HIM, HE CAN SEE YOU! RUN! RUN NOW!' I ran away as fast as I could.

"I was only a child and caved in on myself. I told no one. I wasn't close to my mother; she and I had a turbulent relationship. I didn't think anyone would believe me, so I stayed silent. I had recurring nightmares that the man was executing me; sleeping became a huge problem for me. I lived with the guilt for decades though I didn't realise it then as I was in self-protection mode.

"What made the whole ordeal worse for me was that I had already saved two children's lives (both from drowning) - once when I was eight with my leg in a plaster cast, and again at 14 just before we moved from Sudan to Nigeria.

"My father visited me in 2014 and I asked him whether children went missing back then. He told me they did - sometimes they were sold, other times, stolen. I had firmly locked that memory away until it resurfaced during therapy 35 years later.

"Eventually, we moved to Lagos, Nigeria, where I worked for the British High Commission as a locally engaged employee. At the age of 20, I not only survived a gun attack but I also saved the life of my driver in the process; he would have been executed on the spot had he intervened to stop the event."

If your jaw dropped when reading that, it is hardly surprising.

At the age of 30, Samantha moved to Melbourne, Australia and got married. Sadly, at the age of 31 she lost her daughter, Olivia, during delivery. She became profoundly depressed before her two subsequent children (Josh and Emily) were born. She was apathetic and had stopped caring about life. She realised she needed help to become the mother she wanted to be.

For 10 years she saw a psychotherapist, and it was during these sessions that Samantha was able to let out her pain. She allowed the little girl inside of her - who had been silenced for so long - to be heard. It was a miracle moment when the final piece of the jigsaw puzzle was placed into the tapestry of her life, and she truly healed. She began feeling again, able to express herself in a healthy way. She felt liberated from all the chains that had been holding her back all her life.

She started believing in herself again.

We asked her about the catalyst that led her to realise her own innate abilities and to connect to her best feminine self?

"I had been employed in various sectors, including finance, law enforcement, education, government (Nigeria and Australia), mining, recruitment, retail, security and not-for-profit in an administrative capacity.

"Having had my last child at the age of 40, I wanted to get back into the workforce. I was told that I was too skilled, would get bored and leave - 65 job rejections later, I decided to take matters into my own hands. I investigated what I was good at, and to my complete surprise, I found I was good at public speaking. I entered public speaking competitions, started winning, and in 2014 I competed at the highest level here in Australia.

"By accepting who I was, realising that tapping into an area of my life that hadn't been explored, then building on it by nurturing myself at every level (including self-respect and self-love) I was able to use my newfound ability (to be authentic) in coaching others to become the best version of themselves.

"I feel that it was the fact that I did a lot of hard work to heal my past traumas, (which I kept bringing into the present) that was the turning point for me. By healing, I explored who I was with kindness and compassion when something didn't work out initially. I was able to see those elements of who I was at the time (the elements that I was changing in my exploration of self) as areas that didn't work, rather than as failures. My change in attitude enabled me to then look in a different direction or at a different way of doing things. It's something that I now, in my capacity as mentor and coach, encourage in others.

"I love being a woman! There is a strength to women that is indefinable. How can we put our extraordinary abilities into words? We have the capacity to give life, grow another person inside our bodies. We are nurturers, nurses and teachers to our children. We are warriors for the right to equality. We can multitask wonderfully, for example, hold a business conversation while tending a sick child at the same time. We do not 'babysit' our children; we raise them. Many women get home from work exhausted and go straight into parenting

- often not having a break in between. We have the capacity not only to overcome our own traumas but help others as they face theirs too, and so much more.

"Although there is a great deal of public interest in ensuring more women become leaders, thereby reversing their under-representation in the ranks of power, too many suggested solutions are founded on the misconception that women ought to emulate men." - Harvard Business Review.

"I do not believe that it is necessary for a woman to emulate a man to be a leader or succeed. I have worked with women who have behaved like men in business - the result has been disastrous. They have lacked compassion, reduced staff to tears and ended up having a high turnover of employees. The disappointing element about this is that all of those women were perfectly nice when they didn't have their 'Boss' head on. Each one of them felt a need to be tougher than the men to rise in the ranks.

"In my observations, I recognised a need for us to step into our feminine power as we lead. We should not be afraid to have emotions, but we need to know when to hold them in check when crisis situations arise. As a woman, if we apply all the elements that make us extraordinary, we can use those same things and apply them in a working environment. We are capable of nurturing our staff; listening, understanding and providing the right resources to ensure that they perform to the best of their abilities.

"Women are able to show empathy and communicate with each other, like no other. Why not use those qualities to build strong working relationships, not just in-house but with all stakeholders too? When I worked in the finance industry, I would use these skills to build on and grow my Managing Director's relationships with stakeholders. In so doing, I ensured they wanted to call back and talk, even if it was for the sake of talking. Being friendly and approachable cannot be underestimated in business".

So, what was the catalyst that led her to launch her business?

"To know why **Building Voices Public Speaking** was born, I feel it's important to know my drivers to change career. To call my upbringing challenging would be oversimplifying my experience. My life was one of displacement, violence, and a constant need to adapt to a new environment and culture when living in six countries: Malta, Iran, Africa, Cyprus, the UK and now Australia.

"The parents at my daughter's school who found out that I was an award-winning public speaker approached me for help with their children - telling me that their kids often didn't want to go to school if they had to present in front of classmates. In conversations with teachers, I discovered that they are not fully trained in public speaking though they are trained in the speaking and listening aspects of the curriculum. They aren't taught methods to show a child how to have a confident posture or the practices to control their voice in order to keep an audience's attention.

"By listening to parents, I realised a social need exists for children to develop skills not fully learnt during their formative years at school (outside of debate and drama). There was a practical demand in an area that should better serve our children's needs. As a result, I designed the Junior Public Speaking Program for children from seven to thirteen, and in 2016 Building Voices Public Speaking was launched."

She teaches children confident communication in the classroom, which leads to building self-esteem, encourages positive leadership, and develops important and far-reaching life-skills.

And her challenges in building the business? She admits that having to do everything herself has been difficult at times.

"One of the business setbacks that I have faced is having to do everything myself. I wear all the following hats: coach, CEO, founder, HR, PR, marketing, sales, social media, editor, administrator, bookkeeper and photographer. It used to be exhausting wearing so many hats when I first started out. Through trial and error, I have found that time manangement is key when you are a jack of all trades. I strategically allocate specific times each day and week to cater to the needs of each area. I then mark each task with an 'one', 'two', or 'three' (prioritising them in order) and methodically work through the list. That said, this is an area that I am determined to change this year by upscaling and outsourcing.

"Another challenge I face is that not every parent sees the skills I offer as valuable for their children since they're expecting their child to take over the family business. Interestingly, having coached many children, I can unequivocally say that very few of them want to join a family business. They want to forge their own path in life. I do get so disappointed for the child who wants to continue in my program, but one parent or carer pulls them out. In all honesty, there are no solutions for this. I have tried them all, including offering to coach the child for free. I quickly realised that nothing could make a person change their mind if something does not sit within their value system, even if they can see the difference in their child's confidence as they progress through."

Samantha's coaching business has grown; from working only with children she has expanded her client base to include coaching business leaders and professionals of all types.

"From something that was to be wholly catered only to children, when parents and other professionals heard about the success of my coaching style, they began approaching me to improve their presentation delivery. To date, I have coached CEOs, directors, radio hosts, founders, lawyers, government employees, IT specialists, research scientists, teachers, nurses, photographers … and it won't stop there.

"I've been quite lucky in what I do because people who approach me want to improve their communication style. Many of the women who contact me recognise that to compete with others in business, they need to have their 'story behind the story'. Not just how their business came about, it needs to be much more than that."

Samantha runs workshops of different durations for adults, which focus on developing self-confidence in their presentation abilities. These range from - how to breathe correctly before delivering a speech, organising your thoughts and impromptu speaking, body language, eye contact, gestures, facial expressions, vocal variety, the 'powerful pause', using visual aids, speech writing and delivery. She also offers one-on-one coaching, which is business-focussed and tailored to individual needs.

In 2021, Samantha will launch Building Voices Communication for those who want to take their business to the next level in sharing their untold stories strategically. It will be directed only at adults.

"I plan on holding Storytelling Workshops, where I teach women how to discover and write the 'story behind the story'. Old stories need to be refreshed. By rewriting our stories, we create exciting new opportunities for ourselves, whether as a TEDx presenter, keynote speaker, when interviewed or growing our business to the next level. We shouldn't underestimate the power of storytelling, both written and spoken.

"I want to help those who want to step out of the shadows and who are not afraid to be the heroes of their own lives and stories; where they step into their power and are seen and positioned as an authority in their field. After all, without us and our ideas, we wouldn't have our businesses, and every single woman on this planet deserves to have a voice and be heard."

"A beautiful woman uses her lips for truth, her voice for kindness and good words, her ears for compassion, her hands for charity and her heart for Love." Anne Nwakama.

OFFER:

Claim your 30-minute complimentary session (valued at $150) with Samantha Richards.

She will evaluate your speaking style and how you come across as you speak; do you flow or are you scattered. Let her help you discover what others 'see' and 'hear'. Samantha wants to help you be seen as the authority in your field by fine tuning your communication and storytelling styles.

Email her on samantha_richards@buildingvoices.com.au.

SAMANTHA RICHARDS

Building Voices Communication

M: 0409 110 169
E: samantha_richards@buildingvoices.com.au
W: www.buildingvoices.com.au

Samantha Richards is Australia's top female public speaking coach (Yahoo Finance).

Samantha is an award-winning public speaker who has competed at the highest level in Australia. She is the founder of *Building Voices Public Speaking*; a communication coaching business that works with children and adults to develop lifelong skills as confident communicators. She is currently studying for a Diploma in Counselling and is passionate about helping individuals to be happy and confident when communicating.

In 2021, Samantha will launch *Building Voices Communication* for those who want to take their business to the next level. This platform will help people to share their untold stories and to step into their power to be seen (which will enable them to be positioned as an authority in their field). Building Voices Communication will also be part of her new television series in which she will interview the remarkable people she meets and works with about their journey to success.

"To say I'm excited about what I do is an understatement! I love it when I see someone's communication and storytelling skills develop to the point where they're visibly more confident in how they're coming across." -SR

Ask yourself

1. How many times have you been talking to someone and you've disliked the tone they've used, and this sparked a row? Or perhaps someone has told you not to talk to them in *'that tone of voice'*.

____

____

____

____

2. Have you ever felt that you've suffered from 'imposter syndrome' when you're talking to someone, or you find that you struggle to have those awkward 'money' conversations with people? Do you feel confident in being able to organise your thoughts in such a way that when you answer any question, your listener will understand exactly what you're saying because you speak clearly and answer concisely?

____

____

____

____

Activity

The tone of our voice impacts almost all our conversations. As such, I have a philosophy of *'how someone reacts is exactly how you have been heard'*.

Try saying something that would be classified as mean; for example, I use "You are an idiot!"

Let's practice saying it in three different ways. Look in a mirror (as you speak) to see how your facial expressions affect your tone of voice.

Method 1: Keep your voice staccato and aggressive, emphasising each word. Allow your top lip to curl a bit to create a slight snarl in your tone as if you're angry. Or say "You. Are. An. Idiot!" through gritted teeth. Perhaps, try both ways; but, it should feel harsh, unkind and judgemental.

The likely response you will get from someone will be an immediate downward mood shift. Undoubtedly, an argument would follow.

Method 2: Say the same words in a slightly higher tone, with your eyebrows drawn together, (without being staccato) as if you're astounded by such stupidity. It should feel as though you're patronising the person.

The listener's response would likely be of frustration or irritation.

Method 3: Use the words with a genuine smile on your face. Your vocal tone will automatically lift to sound more friendly; it should feel playful and not as though you're being unkind.

Your listener's response would less likely be combative since your tone isn't judgemental or demeaning.

Finally: Evaluate how each sounded. Ask yourself how you would respond if you were on the receiving end of each tone?

When we actively 'hear' how we sound, we can change our communication style through self-awareness and as a result become more effective when interacting with others.

CATHERINE SKIPERDENE

Director – Connecting Women International

Standing up for women
the world over

> '*Believe that you can*
> *Live like there is no tomorrow*
> *Embrace your passions*
> *Sincerity & kindness in whatever you do*
> *Share your love and purpose*' – CS

My name is Cathy.

To say that I have seen my fair share of life's challenges might seem like an understatement to some:

- I was adopted soon after I was born.

- I was bullied mercilessly at school.

- I have suffered from debilitating illness most of my life.

- As a sick teenager, I was told I would never amount to anything.

- I underwent multiple surgeries and was told I would not live.

- At 18, I was read my last rites by the hospital priest.

- I was told I could never have children - but proved them all wrong. I now have two!

My adoptive parents, Jack and Carmel Skiperdene lived in Newcastle, NSW and they had three sons of their own. I was very fortunate to have been adopted by a wonderful caring and accepting family who were there for me and treated me as their own. I had a wonderful childhood, a good education and supportive parents for whom I am very thankful - but I had health issues from birth and secretly felt guilty that my parents had adopted a 'dud'.

My father did not think I would amount to anything, so I could not wait to prove him wrong! I went above and beyond my dad's expectations, but sadly he was not there to see most of it. I think I started to stand up for myself in high school when I was bullied for two long, miserable years.

I decided I was going to step up and be a voice for the girls that were being bullied, because I did not want to see them go through what I did.

I was always able to talk my way out of anything just by speaking calmly. I really didn't know where the words were coming from, they just came out. I would stick up for others by talking to the bully or attacker, asking how they would feel if they were being bullied. It was quite funny as I was only little, but I just seemed to know what to say to calm everyone down. They respected each other after my talks.

I have done this all my life, automatically stopping fights and giving support to troubled people (even strangers). They seem to be drawn to me. I later discovered my abilities as a psychic counsellor and writer. If I had a problem to solve, I would sit quietly and with paper and pen, close my eyes and ask for

help. I have written many things that have helped myself and others. It is a special gift, which is part of my passion and purpose.

After school I worked with my dad in the family business for a few years (at one of our bookstores), which I enjoyed very much. When we moved to Surfer's Paradise, I got a job as assistant manager for a supermarket but had to leave after I was diagnosed with severe Crohn's Disease, which had been misdiagnosed for years. My illness became progressively worse, to the point where I was read my last rites at the hospital.

I then worked for a company that was part of the launching of the *iPrimus* internet services in Australia. I was part of the corporate team, which worked to introduce the new telecommunication company to companies and businesses, and then residents in South East QLD. I became a member of the training team that went out to talk to residents about the new service. I enjoyed working there, but again had to leave to have another surgery.

It took six months for me to recover, and I took a part-time job as Bar Manager at a Mexican restaurant in Main Beach. I then finally got a full-time job at Myer Pacific Fair running the sporting goods department and assisted with the management of the toy department.

During this time, I became so sick I vomited about 20 times a day but managed it so well that no-one even noticed. I was transferred to various departments but injured my hand and my back from various work accidents. I had to use a walking stick for about 10 years after that.

I got married and built my first house in the same year while still at Myer. Three years later I was 'paid out' for the permanent injuries I received. These injuries stopped me from doing most of the normal things people do. At the age of 29, I was told I would not be able to have children. However, I had my first child, Dustin Kane in 1993. I worked part-time with my husband managing books and doing office work, while being a full-time mum. Dustin was such a good baby. I was blessed.

During this time, I was very sick with Crohn's Disease, and I was in and out of hospital having surgeries. I was told many times that I wasn't going to make it. The condition meant I was unable to work more than a couple of days a week due to ill health. When my son was two and a half, I lost a child through miscarriage but I was focused on having a baby girl. I became pregnant again but was told I would end up in a wheelchair if I continued the pregnancy.

I was *determined* to have my baby girl, and in 1996 my daughter Lauren Ashley was born. I was very lucky to have two beautiful, healthy children and was often referenced at the hospital as the mother of two 'miracle children' during the pregnancy group visits.

It is amazing how we can steer through impossible times with sheer guts and determination, to do things we are told we can't, isn't it?

I went through so many setbacks, though. My ongoing illness meant that I was unable to do what I wanted. It just wasn't possible. This was a challenge in my personal life, of course. With my health problems I could feel fine for about six months and then I would be in hospital for months, this meant I was unable to meet someone who could understand and sympathise with me. I would always get the 'I can't handle your illness' excuse. So, I had a lot of ups and downs. It was hard to feel my Feminessence® and explore the woman that was inside me, when I kept getting put down or rejected one way or another.

My husband and I separated four years later. It was a difficult time for us both. It was really hard being sick and a single mum, as I lost contact with many friends due to the divorce. But I managed to get through it all and started to find myself again. On reflection, I think I went backwards after I was married and had my children, as I was made feel very insignificant. My power started coming back and so did my confidence, when I was asked to stay on at 'Women At Work' (WAW). It affected my life so much that I honestly believed (for the first time in many years), I could do anything and felt proud of who I had become and was becoming.

I had started working on a community jobs program through WAW. This is when I discovered the events industry, which I learned I loved very much. I was trained to create different events to raise money for organisations including The Leukemia Foundation and then later The Gold Coast Centre Against Sexual Violence (for support services and counselling).

After the program finished, I was asked to stay on and work for WAW with their computer training and other programs. I learnt many new skills and was then given the task of going out to the job employment networks to teach staff - helping them to establish a client's particular computer skills needs for different job applications. This was so rewarding as we were helping people return to the workforce.

I continued to work part time with events training and then started to progress with The International Women's Day (IWD) events, expos and awards program. By this time I had developed many skills in the events industry and was becoming more confident. I started to believe in myself again. During the next eight years my colleague and I pretty much ran the IWD festival together. We were given some grants and then later recognised for what we were doing in the community. At the presentation, we were approached to apply for a pilot TV show. We were told that hundreds of applicants had applied, and that they had made a unanimous decision for the first time. It was an exciting time - we were putting shows together about everyday people and topics like cyber-bullying, health and online dating. We learned a lot about TV and what it takes to produce and write a TV show, which would entertain a large audience.

I had also been assisting with bookkeeping and office work at a car dealership, for about 10 years. I can now value and sell cars with the knowledge I have acquired. I can even test drive sale vehicles and can pick out specific noises to determine what problems a car has, if any.

I was asked to assist a former colleague from WAW, to work with her as Assistant Operations Manager for the Gold Coast Show. After about six years I eventually became the Operations Manager at the Gold Coast Show. Due to the stresses of the position, I ended up in hospital one week after the show ended, for the last two consecutive years that I worked there. I had been working 18 hours a day running around preparing for the three-day show, making sure all 350 exhibitors were happy.

I had totally used up everything I had in me.

I was kept in hospital for a month, and they thought I was going to die. As a result of the multiple surgeries I had to have, my intestine was reduced to the smallest size that is needed to survive - which means I cannot have any more surgeries. After learning this, I decided to retire from the show as it was not worth risking my health any longer.

I then continued with WAW for four months a year, putting on the IWD events and the Youth Recognition Awards Programs. Recognising amazing women and girls from our community and schools was so rewarding - most of them were humble and did not know why they were being celebrated.

With a vision to grow the Official International Women's Day Festival and events, Connecting Women International was then created – its purpose is to honour women and young people in leadership through mentoring programs. This organisation connects people from around the world through online platforms, to share knowledge and experience courage and determination so we can better equip the young women leaders of our future.

I am Founder and Director of Connecting Women International Inc., which is a non-profit organisation. We took over the rights to The Official International Women's Day Festival (held annually for the past 26 years) for both the Youth Leadership Awards, Breakfast and Mentoring Forum and the Open Leadership Awards and Celebration Lunch/Gala Dinner for the Gold Coast, Northern NSW and Brisbane Regions.

Since taking control in 2018, I have expanded the Connecting Women International events to include a mentoring program for the youth nominated each year by their schools. 'The Mentors' are women who are leading the way in prominent positions, from a diverse range of careers and industry as well as selfless amazing women contributing to our communities.

Our mission is to provide a platform to educate, recognise, celebrate and inspire women and youth within a supportive community, enabling them to experience quality change, break free of their limits and realise their purpose and vision. Our purpose is to help guide life decisions, influence behaviour, shape goals, offer a sense of direction and create meaning.

On the 18th of March 2021, we celebrated our Official International Women's Day Festival Youth Leadership Awards and our mentoring forum for the very first time as an online event. Schools from Northern NSW, Gold Coast and Brisbane regions participated and nominated students for the leadership awards. We had some amazing women speakers and panellists from the Gold Coast and other parts of Australia, Papua New Guinea, Qatar and Jamaica. The topics covered were focused on leadership and overcoming challenges. Panel discussions covered careers in sport, the arts and leadership for young women.

It was about celebrating guts and determination!

Connecting Women International will be launching our annual subscription this year. The subscription benefits will include connecting with countries around the world via podcast, video interviews on topics that affect us worldwide. Members will be able to share knowledge, ideas, experience, advice and create lasting connections with some inspirational people from around the world, while interacting personally with each other.

Our mission is to provide an unsurpassed opportunity (post-Covid), for all subscribers in the global community, to make lasting business and social connections. We are giving people a platform to share their expertise, experience and advice with like-minded individuals. This connection will also enable members to contribute to our youth mentoring program – providing local and international mentors for participants.

This is my purpose and my vision.

Women have a major role to play in the business world, as we have different qualities from men. We tend to be more nurturing, patient and caring of other peoples' feelings. We are more empathetic. Women have great people and time management skills. I also believe women listen better to clients, patients and workmates. I do think that women need to stop competing with each other in business and their personal lives, and to start supporting each other and lifting each other up. I see it all the time. In the workplace, I believe a combination of men and women make up the perfect team. Life is not a competition. If we all work together, only then will we have equality in all aspects of life.

I have experienced many challenges in my life. I believe we should help our youth, so they do not have to go through the things I went through. Hopefully, this will become a ripple effect and our future young adults will shine with confidence, self-belief, compassion, and lead by example to a better future and equality.

After my many illnesses, I should not really be here, but my passion and purpose have helped me through. I needed to be here for my two children; they are my main driving force. After nearly dying so many times, I now truly believe my purpose is to help our youth become adults with confidence, self-belief and the ability to cope with challenges head on, stop bullying and have the tools to combat anxiety and depression.

In 2014, I met the love of my life and we have been together for seven years. Jeffrey O'Connor proposed to me in November of 2020, and we look forward to growing old together. Between us, we have four children; Jeff's two girls and my son Dustin (who is now 27) and Lauren (24). For the very first time I have someone that believes in me and was there for me when I was sick and in hospital. We are best friends, partners and we love each other very much. We have been through so much together with his divorce, my health issues and children - but thankfully, we have come through the other side.

I love my crafts and art painting is my release for stress. I am the kind of person who is always trying something new. Gardening and making terrariums are a passion of mine and I love being in the outdoors with my fiancé. We are out on the water most weekends and we spend a lot of time fishing and camping. Dancing is also something I have always loved to do as I find it is my way of releasing tension and stress.

What motivates me is that I *actually wake up* every morning, still alive! I have two beautiful, miracle, healthy children and a beautiful, supportive fiancé. I am able to help our youth, women and men feel self-love again; I can help provide tools to combat anxiety and depression, and contribute towards creating an anti-bullying, anti-abuse (sexual / mental / physical) society.

I am up to my 15th life so far. I now know my purpose and my passion - and I am going for it!

Just watch this space!

CATHERINE SKIPERDENE

Connecting Women International

M: 0466 918 998
E: info@connectingwomeninternational.com

Cathy Skiperdene has been a passionate advocate for women for over two decades, supporting women (and men) with building confidence and self-esteem, while equipping them with the essential skills required to successfully re-enter the work force.

In addition to working with Women at Work, Cathy has been an essential part in establishing the International Women's Day Gold Coast Festival, which has been recognising women and youth for outstanding contributions to the school community and society in general for more than 20 years.

Cathy has worked in the retail, hospitality, building, marketing and events industries. Working in various management roles with organisations such as Myer and the Gold Coast Show.

In 2018 she founded Connecting Women International, and is also the owner of WAW and the OIWD Festival. Cathy has continued to grow the festival by including much needed mentoring programs for youth. These programs involve enabling female mentors from industry, business and community to share their experiences, leadership, wisdom and career pathways, and provide tools for the participants, which better equip them to enter the big wide world as confident, self-loving and determined young women. Connecting Women International is also creating a platform for women globally to connect and share experience, culture and wisdom.

Outside of work Cathy loves painting, crafts, dancing and gardening for relaxation. Cathy spends a lot of time with her mother who has Alzheimer's Disease. She enjoys time with her fiancé Jeff on their boat fishing and camping most weekends. She also loves spending time with her grown up children, both son & daughter and Jeff's girls - she is so proud of them all. Cathy enjoys traveling and exploring our wonderful land, loves meeting new people and learning new things. Cathy believes we can all create a ripple effect (each and every day of our lives) simply with an act of kindness, a smile or a complement to a stranger, and this will create a better and equal future for us all.

OFFER:

If you would like information on leadership, mentoring programs and connecting women globally we would love to hear from you.

Please contact us directly at
info@connectingwomeninternational.com

Photography © Professional images by Studio Republic www.studiorepublic.com.au

Activity

1. What were the challenges that impacted your life?

____

____

____

____

2. What does the word 'leadership' mean to you?

____

____

____

____

3. What have you done to support and inspire others?

____

____

____

____

4. What is your passion and purpose?

____

____

____

____

Unstoppable. Unapologetic.

> *'Be true to yourself and the rest will take care of itself'* – SS

What does Feminessence® mean to Shantelle Saiville?
It is understanding your role as *you*, who you are and what you want to become in your life as an individual. This really comes down to what fulfils you and gives your life a sense of meaning, purpose and flow.

What does Feminessence® mean to Shantelle Saiville? It is understanding your role as you, who you are and what you want to become in your life as an individual. This really comes down to what fulfils you and gives your life a sense of meaning, purpose and flow.

Shantelle understands the nuances of being a woman. She has always wanted to lead others by example - to inspire them to follow their heart's desires. She has explored many avenues in her life as a marketing manager, TV show host, a public speaker and more. She has never been afraid to try something new, and because of that she understands how to help others to discover and truly relish their true identity, however long it has been hidden.

"I have always felt connected to the feminine and the unseen, but didn't fully understand it. I just embraced my imagination, and as I got older these things started coming to fruition. I was born in central Canada and grew up in the prairie province of Saskatchewan. I spent much of my time with my grandparents on their farm. Although we didn't have a lot of money, I was full of love and imagination. I also had an imaginary family, and deep down inside I knew there was more to life than what was in front of me.

When I was 18, I took a one-year working holiday to Australia, which had been my dream since I was five. As soon as I landed, I knew that I was exactly where I was meant to be. Over the years I completed a marketing degree, was a marketing manager of an Audi car dealership, was a PA to a multimillionaire (I was like the girl from the movie The Devil Wears Prada) and ran a corporate gifts business. All were interesting and fun, but deep down I knew I was destined for something else.

I went on to pursue/explore coaching, speaking, many wellness modalities and even competed as a fitness model (to demonstrate physically what is possible when you put your mind to something). After my husband's contract took us to Hawaii, I landed my dream role of having my very own show in Hawaii called the SaviChiX Show - where I interviewed the most inspiring people that I knew to show others what is possible when you believe in yourself. The guests on my show would share their journeys and how they got to where they were.

Growing up, I was a rule follower and always well-behaved. One exception was the time when I was about six years old. My mom and grandma took my sister and me to a family karaoke restaurant. I'd watch a lot of the Mickey Mouse Club show on television and thought it could be my chance 'to get discovered'. I tried to leave the house in spandex, a crop top and little heels, but much to my disappointment, I was told to go and change. I ignored them, packed a bag, and snuck it with me in the car. When the time came for me to sing, I quickly went to the bathroom, changed into my little rockstar outfit and went straight to the stage. My mom and grandma were horrified when they saw me up there in the outfit I was told not to wear! To this day, they think it was one of the funniest things ever. When I reflect on it now, I understand that even back then I knew what it meant to be truly self-expressed and unstoppable - even for a people-pleasing rule-follower!

Since then, I have had two incredible children, Lagatha (who is four) and Ethan (who is one-and-a-half). They have opened my mind and heart so much.

I think the catalyst that led me to being my best feminine self was embarking on a Feminine Power course and the birth of my son Ethan. There was a sudden calmness in my heart, and I surrendered to and embraced the true gift it was to be a mother and what an important role it is.

I experienced this with my daughter too, of course, but still felt like I should be 'doing more'. It felt like 'just being a mom' wasn't contributing to society. I constantly had this voice in my head saying you are educated, have so much experience and have come so far, you should really be doing more. When I stepped into my best feminine self, it was like I no longer had anything to prove and that I was worthy being just who I am. I had clarity on 'why I am here' and gave myself full permission to shine in my light.

I started doing less and BEING MORE. The more I showed up as ME the more I would attract what is TRUE TO ME and synchronicity.

The more I felt worthy and deserving, the more others reflected this to me. I started really listening and following my inner guidance and knowing. It was a time that through self-exploration and expression I could feel what it really felt like to be me - a powerful yet graceful women. And yes, wearing makeup and dressing to express my feminine essence really gave me confidence in my feminine power and initiated my self-worth.

I came to the realisation that I decide what success is - not other people. By living in accordance with my values for flow and fulfilment, I was able to let go of the need to prove or justify anything. I gave myself permission to truly live for me. Any problems or opposition I faced were the result of my old thoughts creeping in; thinking I should be doing more and trying to 'hustle'. I am now able to recognise this and shift back into my feminine power. Meditation helps me enormously with this!

Learning not to react is something that still takes a conscious effort. I practise speaking up for what matters to me from a centred, worthy place. The easiest way I find to do this is keeping the focus on myself and keeping things in my 'lane'.

I now have no desire to control, be liked or a people-pleaser. I show up unapologetically as myself, so that my real tribe and those who I'm here to serve can see me and step into their power too. This liberated way of living is very freeing.

What's true for me right now, is being present as a mom and embracing and nurturing my children. When I nurture my children, I feel my own soul being nurtured - anything else that I can fit in these days is a bonus!

Even though women have come so far in terms of where we were, we are still considered the main caretakers of our children and our homes.

It was only when I became a mother and experienced this for myself, that I could appreciate what an important role it is. I really feel that society undervalues this role by putting unrealistic expectations on mothers. This leaves us feeling torn and confused. It seems as though as soon as your child turns one (or even earlier) you are expected to go back to 'work' and be a super mom that can 'do it all'. This puts pressure on mothers to feel like we need to go back to work, even though deep down we yearn to be with our baby/child. This isn't just a financial pressure it is also mental and emotional.

After I had my first child I went through a phase of not knowing what I wanted to do 'professionally' at all. All I wanted to do was be with my daughter. After my son was born, I started really leaning into my feminine essence and flow. I came to realise that my true power was in my ability to recognise my worth and the importance of my role as a mother.

Women can do it all, but don't or shouldn't have to. We are no more or less worthy if we have a successful career, our house is clean, or our children are 'perfect'. What matters is how we feel and if we are being true to ourselves!

Being a mother comes at a cost, but it's a question of values to me. I am prepared to have less financial reward (for a small amount of time) for something that is important to me. My top value - and what truly fulfils me – is being a mother.

When you see your worth, others see it too.

I now realise that I can do both but only with the majority of my focus on my family because they are my priority. I know that every day I wake up, dress up and am the best version of myself, that is progression. Right now that (combined with the small steps that I am taking towards my vision and mission) is what keeps me in alignment.

When I try to do too much and take the focus off my family, my life ends up in chaos. I know better now. I flow with what feels best in each moment. I really believe when your attention is split between too many places, the result is the feeling that you are failing at everything.

Our children won't be young for long and I know that our time spent with them is invaluable. When we can make an impact on our children, we can make a difference in the world.

Of course, women have much to contribute in business. That goes without saying. Women can make a great contribution by working for themselves, being entrepreneurs or working for other female businesswomen. By understanding our own value and self-worth and tapping into our feminine power, we can make a great impact in male dominated industries (by bringing out the best in our colleagues).

I believe women's special contributions are our abilities to create, to see in colour (rather than black and white) and not only listen to others but to truly hear them - using this input for the greater good. What holds us back is confidence, self-doubt and self-worth, not being in alignment with our true self and not listening to or using our voice. Up the wrong ladder, so to speak!

So, how did I start my business?

Nine years ago (after doing a lot of mindset work and courses) I decided to move out of the corporate world, take a leap of faith and create SaviLife, something that would make a difference in people's lives, the community and the world.

Though it has changed its shape, form and evolved over the years, the core message remains the same - 'Live the Life you Love' (A Life True to You).

I felt so many people were disconnected from their true selves. Too much of peoples' social interaction revolved around drinking alcohol and going to bars.

I wanted to create something different that would be fun and empower women to try new things. I formed a modern-day sisterhood, which I called SaviChiX - where we could grow and achieve our big dreams together.

It started with me coaching people one-on-one. I hosted SaviChiX events - everything from horse polo to stand-up paddle boarding, yoga, personal styling events and even an exclusive event with Human Behaviour Specialist, Dr John Demartini.

It is amazing what can happen when you go out and try something new, spend time with like-minded people or reconnect with something that you used to love doing. These simple get togethers began transforming lives.

One of the women was working in a job in an industry that she no longer enjoyed. After just one introduction to horse polo, she was hooked and started lessons every weekend. This brought her joy and helped her attract and land a new job that she loved.

Another young woman had never been into fitness or even used a skipping rope. Amazingly, she went on to finding her true passion in fitness; doing marathons, ironman competitions and even climbing to the Mount Everest base camp!

I went on to becoming a speaker, blogger, and continued to build the SaviChiX brand (helping to inspire girls to be themselves, believe in themselves and follow their dreams) and eventually hosted the SaviChiX Show. I was fortunate to interview a variety of inspirational careers including professional mermaid, stunt woman, clothing designer, and many more.

Since becoming a mother I have shifted gears and focused on being more, learning more, improving my parenting style and expanding my mind-set. It has been a great time to reflect and upskill. During this time I have embarked on a Fingerprint for Success: People Leader and Entrepreneurship Coaching course as well as a Feminine Power Leadership course. I'm excited to start my leadership project in the coming months with the aim to have my Feminine Power Leadership Certification by this time next year, if not sooner!

I have explored more coaching and facilitation techniques and found my love and true gift in Intuitive Alignment Coaching. This along with books, mini courses, podcasts and audios have kept me connected to my business and purpose. I really believe my purpose is to light people up and help them live in alignment with their true selves; to open their eyes, minds and hearts to the abundance this world has to offer.

When people believe in themselves and give themselves permission to live a life that is true to them, anything is possible!

Although I am not entirely sure what's next for me, I do know that I love people, connecting, collaborating, community, creating, hosting, speaking and coaching. I especially love connecting people to the essence of their being, finding out what matters most to them and helping them discover their priorities so that they live their lives in alignment with their values.

In the end, it is about living whatever is true to YOU, not what others expect of you or the unrealistic expectations you put on yourself.

I want to help women feel good about themselves and have a sense of purpose and identity, while keeping their focus on their family - if that is what they long to do.

Whatever it is that you choose to do, know that I believe in you!

Finally, I think the essence of being a woman is our heart, intuition, creativity, empathy and nurturing qualities. It's our ability to feel deeply and to hold space for others too. This differs from the typical structure, power, control, rational, task orientated, results driven/'must do' traits that we might find in men.

The feminine is graceful yet strong, beautiful and open. It is the ability to feel and trust what cannot be seen but only felt when deeply connected to it. I think the *characteristics that define femininity are soft, flowing, fluid, empathetic, caring and kind.*

And that is what I strive to be.

'Be true to yourself and the rest will take care of itself' - Shantelle.

OFFER:

If you would like more information about Shantelle, to collaborate, join her community or book a coaching session, visit

www.savilife.com or www.savimumma.com

SHANTELLE SAIVILLE

Savimumma, SaviLife and SaviChiX

E: hello@savimumma.com
W: www.savimumma.com & www.savilife.com

Do Less ... Be More ...

Shantelle helps new mums transition into and embrace motherhood, while having a sense of self, purpose and confidence...

She is passionate about making the new mum experience and journey an enjoyable one. Shantelle also helps mums create lifestyle businesses that are an extension of who they are.

Known as the 'Stay-at-home mom who rarely stays at home', Shantelle is dedicated to her family but knows she is more than 'just a mom'.

Shantelle embraces her mom life by being active with her children and simplifying her life to make it enjoyable.

'Cool, Calm and Connected' is the type of mom she strives to be...

From being a Marketing Manager to speaking on the stages of wellness expos and girls' schools, and even hosting her own TV show, Shantelle has enjoyed seeing many of her dreams turn into reality. She now feels most at home and fulfilled being and embracing her mumma life.

Shantelle thrives on connection, and she is creating a community of like-minded mums who want to be the best they can be for themselves and their family.

We're not just mummas...

We're SaviMummas...

Learning, Glowing and Growing together!

Activity

My life now is all about staying in alignment with myself by focusing on my values. It is less about the highs and lows, and more about going with what flows; doing what speaks to me and answering the call of what excites my spirit. It's all about simplifying, clarifying and strategising. That is how I love to help people.

Here are a few of the simple things to get you started doing the same:

- Become clear on who you truly are.

- What do you truly want?

- Clear your closets and clutter for clarity.

- Try to only wear what makes you feels really good about yourself (even if it means wearing it often)!

- What does abundance mean to you?

- Define what success means to you.

- Be grateful for what you already have.

- If what you are 'looking for' is already present in your current life, focus on it so you can receive more of it.

- Try something new or go back to something you used to do!

It's about making your life (and even business if you have or wish to have one) an extension of who you are. People are attracted to who you are being. When you are being the truest version of you, the results are you feel more alive, aligned, connected and self-expressed.

Teaching women how to **re-capture pleasure in their lives.**

> *'Pleasure is found through our sensual bodies.*
> *Beauty unfolds with positive attention.*
> *Wild is daring to be fully expressed'* – JA

Mine is a story of conformity, rebellion, and of releasing attachment to both. It is a story of freedom.

Being born a girl in my first nature was a blessing and a privilege beyond my wildest knowing, a fact that has taken me many decades to fully appreciate.

In that first nature I was connected to what some call the Goddess, others the Divine, or as my favourite teacher calls it, the Great Pussy in the Sky!

As a young girl I accessed that connection through dancing. Moving my body felt good and (although I was not familiar with the idea at that age) it offered me a way home to myself and the feminine parts of me. I experienced flow, grace, ease, joy and a sense of agency and power.

Slowly I began to adopt my second nature (as I came to understand) and appreciate that being the 'good girl' and pleasing others offered me love and attention.

I was the first born of two sisters, to loving and adoring parents.

I was praised as a child for being clever, talented and (dare I say it) pretty. I was outgoing because I believed that was expected of me and made others happy.

I was entered into baby shows and competitions, and competitive dancing from a young age. I grew up believing that winning equated with success, and that my achievements made me worthwhile.

The expectation I felt growing up was that I was intelligent and that I was going to do the things that my parents never had the opportunity to do, most importantly to complete my education. I grew up believing that my mind would be my saviour.

Alongside my 'good girl' persona sat a growing rebel who was often labelled as strong-willed (as I began to increasingly push back against this notion).

The trigger for my rebellion? Perhaps it was the abuse and traumatic personal experiences in my formative years that continued to show up right through into my early adulthood. Perhaps it was the little voice inside me that whispered (just loud enough) to let me know she was there - and that I was not alone.

By the age of 12 I no longer wanted to be a girl. I did not yet fully recognise the Patriarchal system in which I was being raised; the system I saw played out in the lives of my family and of those people around me, in the school and the church I attended. I did however recognise that I was at a disadvantage as a girl and decided that being a boy would bring an easier path in life. I cut my hair, started dressing like a boy, played with boys, rejected my mother and her love and attention, and began to strongly associate with my father and in turn with the masculine.

Although I was successful in my pursuits in the creative arts through dance, and excelled in my studies throughout my teenage years, it was the wrong teachings, cultural injustices and the judgements and pressure of competing both on and off the stage that stripped me of my self-worth. The abuse I experienced took on different forms and faces, and I chose to increasingly live in the masculine and, as a result, shut down my feelings.

But I didn't break.

In fact, my strength became my identity. I hid my struggles from the world and from my loved ones and tried to sort it out for myself. The more I stepped into my masculine, the less open I became to receiving support. In those times when I did reach out, the support always seemed to fall short as it was too confronting for others to face. And so, I lived in constant shame and disapproval of myself.

I spent these years believing that my rebellion was allowing me to live in my own power. In effect it achieved the opposite. I grabbed the next boy, (and as I aged) the next man that came along - no matter how destructive. I slowly gave away more and more of my power, never slowing down long enough to be able to explore myself from the inside out. I searched outside myself, believing I needed fixing.

Those years tested and grew my resilience. Despite the knockdowns I contained the turmoil, the grief, the anger and the resentment. I managed an outward appearance of success. But there was something within me, something intangible but also very real that kept me going and growing ... a knowing, a remembering, a hint, that there was more to be discovered.

Paradoxically, alongside the struggle I had become so adept at hiding, life and opportunities came easily to me. In my earlier adulthood, I was sought after in the professional world; successfully securing positions I interviewed for and advancing in my career as an Executive Assistant. I excelled again at studying, this time in Criminal Justice and Social Work. I was abundant in friendships and relationships.

Despite this ease, discovering my essential power as a woman came slowly and gradually, and with a series of catalysts that built upon and provided the foundation for the next.

My first conscious experience of stepping into my essential power as a woman was at aged 39 with the birth of my son. The process of creating and giving birth enabled me to reconnect into the wisdom of my body in ways that I had not experienced.

However, I was completely unprepared for the demands of motherhood and I found being a new mother difficult.

Both my son and I experienced health challenges, and alongside this he unknowingly held up a mirror for me to see all the ways I still disapproved of myself. In striving to be the perfect mother I fell into constant worry and feared that I was not showing up in all the ways I needed to ensure his happiness. These self-imposed struggles began to take a big toll on my physical, emotional and mental health. I lived in constant exhaustion. It affected my relationship with my husband and with the people around me, whom I began to shut out because they could not keep up with my artificial expectations of perfection.

Weighing under 45 kilos (much of which was breast milk) I gradually came to the realisation that I had taken the expectations that were given to me as child and was in the process of passing them onto my own.

I began a search for support and discovered the philosophy of Aware Parenting - where all parts of our human experience are welcome, all emotions are valid, and play is seen as vital to wellbeing and attachment. As I embraced this philosophy in my parenting, I began to 'reparent' myself and truly connect into my innate power as a woman. I connected to my own inner loving mother, which gave me permission to love being a woman and to love being a mother. Alongside this I discovered a community of sisterhood and unconditional support through listening partnerships and safe spaces.

I found that I wanted to live with less seriousness and connect back to my playfulness. Enter the practice of Laughter Yoga. Unexpectedly, through intentional laughter I discovered a gateway into my spirituality. And that may sound funny because laughter can be seen as frivolous. There was nothing frivolous in how this practice enabled me to loosen the grip on my problems. It quite literally cracked me open - and I began effortlessly playing my joy key and adopting a positive mindset. Again, I connected into an amazing community filled with incredible women who inspired me. I started to experience relationships with women and men in different ways. I found greater permission to be myself, to begin to let go of my story of being 'too much' and I felt welcome to bring the essence of my feminine creativity to this practice.

Intentional laughter was such a catalyst for me because it took me into a body mind practice where I was able to reconnect to the wisdom within my body. I had spent so much time in my head, which had not served me well. I knew I was onto something transformational and I wanted more!

Next to find me was Qoya, an embodied movement practice, which became an even bigger catalyst for reconnecting me to my body and my feminine power.

I began to practice Qoya daily and slowly, bit by bit, through moving with meaning I began to tap deeper into my essence as a woman, and the essence of the feminine as being wise, wild and free. I decided to journey into teaching Qoya to other women, guiding them into reconnecting with their feminine through a fun and meaningful 'way back home' to their bodies and the pleasure of movement.

Through Qoya I met a woman who would go on to become one of my biggest inspirations and now co-creator in the work I share with women. Her introduction into the world of pleasure greatly impacted my journey of reclamation back into my whole self, back into my feminine and back into my enjoyment in being a woman. Through her work I learned about the School of The Womanly Arts and discovered the best-selling author of Pussy: *A Reclamation*.

I embraced the rules of 'Cliteracy' and I discovered that beauty through positive attention, being kind to myself and practising relentless self-compassion, are the surest ways to access my feminine self.

My teachers have taught me that through reconnecting with the most sacred parts of my body as my power source (through turn-on and pleasure) that I am able to step out of any notion of victimhood and into my power as a woman, willing to fully claim my birthrights. I have learnt how to stop giving my power away to those outside of myself and have a deep understanding that if I am not owning my own power, then someone else is.

I now share these teachings with other women and co-founded the Wild Beauty and Pleasure Alliance alongside two incredible Sister Goddesses.

Together we lead women back to their whole selves through curiosity and pleasure research, sharing tools and practices that give women choice and take each other higher, championing and role modelling the power of raw and real sisterhood.

As a practicing Master Neuro Linguistic Programming Practitioner and Time-Line Therapist my essential power as a woman has come full circle. I no longer sit in the reasons for my life. I have come to know that although I was not responsible for any of the trauma I experienced or the things that happened to me, I can take charge of my own results and create my own destiny. I have developed a deep relationship with my unconscious mind and have been able to find the positive learnings in past experiences - I call this taking radical responsibility for oneself. I now have access to and allies in my whole self ... mind, body and spirit ... and this wholeness creates the woman I am becoming.

I have faced many challenges in my life.

I have experienced what most women face being raised in a Patriarchal society; standards and conditioning that are designed to keep us small, keep our voices contained and keep a lid on ourselves; to distrust ourselves and our bodies; to disapprove of ourselves; to control us by dictating we control ourselves.

I faced the relentless expectations of success accompanied by push, strive, grasp and perfection. I believed that I needed to follow a linear path through life without consideration or recognition for the powerful feminine experience of expansion and contraction in creation.

As I have stepped further outside these expectations and systems, I have faced judgement not only from men but also from other women. Sisters who are unfortunately still caught in the beliefs that we need to compete and that there is a scarcity of resources for women to share. I have witnessed women get angry when their situation becomes clearer, when they are called to their own awakening of the self-disapproval they have been carrying around.

I also accept that many of the setbacks I faced were self-imposed.

Today I overcome setbacks, problems and opposition through truth telling, through radical and unnerving curiosity and through allowing vulnerability in sharing my story. I choose to find joy and pleasure not only in the ease-filled moments, but also in the fight to bring women back to the reclamation of their full selves, and in the fight to invite women into the truth of the Patriarchal systems that still dominate and influence our way of life.

I see myself as a change-maker and a visionary in leading women to create new systems. In encouraging women to make different choices and demand systems where these choices are honoured.

I choose to no longer be held back by limitations, glass ceilings, to toe the line, or to see myself as a victim to these.

Freedom comes to me in embracing my true expression, not in an *'away from'* energy where I externalise and look to things outside myself for answers. Rather in a *'towards'* energy as a whole woman who can fight for what she believes in. My essential power does not come from me being anti-masculine, but from embracing the feminine and being ruthlessly true to myself.

I have chosen to consciously uncouple from my marriage without animosity, co-parent from a space of love and respect, adopt a philosophy of parenting outside the norm where I welcome my son to feel his emotions, follow his choices and encourage his true expression. I home educate him in the belief that he does not need to be raised in an institution to find his own purpose in life.

For over 20 years I have chosen to work in an entrepreneurial space where I have created my own businesses. I have now found my voice championing that part of a woman's anatomy that I know (from personal experience) is the surest way home to our whole selves as women.

I believe in my innate birthright to pleasure.

I trust in the wisdom stored within my own body.

I connect to my innate essence of being wild and free, to the creative expression of movement and to my senses and my sensual body.

I believe the feminine essence permeates everything that exists. That the feminine aspect of every person is necessary for us to be internally inclusive.

I choose to explore femininity as the purest form of feminine expression, acknowledging that all women and men can benefit from a balance of both inherent energies.

Femininity for me is defined by constant change and includes characteristics of feeling, openness, kindness, generosity, wisdom, support, community, connection, flexibility, compassion, fertility, intuition, patience, nurturance and care, sustainability and growth.

Regardless of one's gender identity we ALL birth something - whether that is an idea, a friendship, a business plan, or a family. We can ALL appreciate delight and beauty.

Masculine energies are linear and include characteristics such as focus, logic, discipline, rationality, action, production, purpose, vision, strength and leadership.

We can ALL benefit from a healthy representation of the masculine, where we can be strong but gentle.

In this way we can ALL commit to a fairer, kinder, gentler and more empathetic way of being with each other.

Personally, and professionally, I desire to be the change I want to see in the world.

My signature coaching program, RECLAIM YOUR PLEASURE SELF, combines some of the most powerful tools on the planet in both mind and embodiment practices. I skilfully and intuitively guide a woman to water the seeds of creation that live within her and to bring them to life; to live fully aligned with her values and create future goals to open the gateways to her greatest desires, and to take love in action. To break free of her limiting beliefs and conditioning and to become rich in positive attention for herself.

Every woman deserves to:

- Get to know her body.

- Connect with others.

- Speak freely.

- Expand her awareness and capacity for what is possible.

- Participate in ritual and ceremony.

- Value her whole self in body, mind and spirit.

- Be witnessed, celebrated and appreciated.

All my offerings (from one-on-one coaching and therapy to online and in-person group programs) are created in the belief that pleasure is found through our sensual bodies. That beauty equals positive attention. That wild is daring to be fully expressed.

The success of my offerings comes from the positive experiences of the women who have journeyed with me. This includes that they …

Feel safe and held in sharing their story and supported in the process.

Find the experience to be incredibly freeing and enriching.

Feel lighter within themselves.

Feel confident stepping onto new paths.

Feel liberated in mind, body and spirit.

See possibilities where they could not previously.

Find the 'ifs' and 'buts' and self-made roadblocks considerably dimmer.

Have been delighted with the insights and clarity they have uncovered.

Have been able to understand and unleash their feminine energy to assist in attracting huge abundance into their lives.

Feel peaceful and rested.

Look 25 years younger!"

Jennifer's life-long journey of self-discovery has enabled her to guide others on their own pathways to pleasure.

And that is *her* joy.

"The woman you are becoming will cost you people, relationships, spaces and material things. Choose her over everything." Unknown.

OFFER:

Book your place in Jen's signature coaching program

RECLAIM YOUR PLEASURE SELF and RECEIVE a
20% DISCOUNT when you quote 'FEMINESSENCE®'.

JENNIFER ANNETTE

The Joy Space Pty Ltd

M: 0419 100 533
E: jennifer@thejoyspace.com.au
W: www.wildbeautypleasure.com

A woman deserves to feel good in her body, and empowered in her thoughts and desires.

With my body as a guide and pleasure as my compass, I have liberated myself from conformity and rebellion, and discovered a freedom in redefining success.

I swapped a multi-million-dollar business (of 25 years) that no longer served me for a different type of entrepreneurship - founding several purpose-driven businesses that now feed my soul and prosperity.

I have taught hundreds of women how to reconnect with their body and harness the power of their unconscious mind.

I live in Melbourne with my loving partner, home educate my amazing son, and enjoy being in my garden every day.

Jen is a Master Neuro Linguistic Programming (NLP) Practitioner, Time Line Therapist®, Certified Qoya Embodiment Teacher, Laughter for Wellbeing Facilitator and a sought-after presenter in the wellbeing space.

Her signature programs successfully guide a woman in healing her relationship with self and body, and show her how to re-capture pleasure.

Jen is co-founder of The Wild Beauty and Pleasure Alliance - a collaboration of female activists who trust in the power of pleasure and the freedom found in remembering our innate beauty, wisdom and wildness. Jen offers online and in-person, individual and group programs, retreats and masterclasses including the wildly successful, A Book Club With A Difference.

She is also co-creator and host of the Podcast 'Pussy Tales', which shares women's stories of their reclamation of their whole selves.

Activity

Slowing down, taking a breath and bringing your awareness to your body.

1. First notice your posture and how you are positioned in the space around you. Ask yourself, 'What do I feel in my body right now?' 'Where do I feel it?' Find three words to describe this to yourself.

____

____

____

____

2. What do you notice in this moment through your senses? What do you see, hear, smell, taste, feel?

____

____

____

____

3. Does this connection to your senses bring you pleasure?

____

____

____

____

4. Is there something, (no matter how small) you can do in this moment (by bringing positive attention to yourself) to allow your experience to be more pleasurable? Perhaps you might sip your tea a little slower, rub your hands together, feel the sensations of the earth beneath your feet, close your eyes and gently circle your neck, gently cradle your chin in your hands, run your fingers through your hair.

____

____

____

____

Now celebrate yourself!

5. Have you ever experienced your wild essence through feeling fully expressed? Shuffle your music and begin to move your body with the first track that plays. Every movement (from a gentle sway to a wild shake) is a guide back into your body.

____

____

____

____

6. Do you notice a shift in your state? When in the height of the sensations you are experiencing, you can anchor the feeling into your body by bringing your thumbs to connect with the pad of another finger. The more you do this, the stronger the anchor will become.

____

____

____

____

226

CAROL ARAVENA

Founder - Diamond-Light

Metaphysical Practitioner, B.Msc. Intuitive Quantum Healer, Certified Reiki Master, Magnetic Mind Method Coach, NLP Practitioner, NES Health Practitioner, Sacred Rainbow Colour Therapist

Creating a
life you love

'Don't let someone dim your light simply because it's shining in their eyes' – Unknown

I was born the youngest of six in a lower-class family in Valparaiso, Chile.

I have only a handful of memories of my native land, as I was only four when my parents made the bold move to migrate to Australia. It was only as an adult with a family of my own that I appreciated the courage and tenacity my parents had leaving behind family, friends and country. My Dad was the only one in the family that could speak self-taught English.

My nearest sibling is a brother who is four years older than I am - and we remain close to this day. The rest of my siblings were older, engaged or married and so they weren't really an integral part of my childhood. I started school without being able to speak a single word of English, with dark skin amongst fair skinned Aussie kids. This was the beginning of a lifetime of being different. We moved a lot, so I was always the new kid with the wrong uniform. As a result, I remember being a lonely, shy and timid child. My little portable radio became my best companion. Friendships outside of school were not supported unless they lived next door. Sleepovers and school camps were never an option.

My mother had unusual and dysfunctional views and perceptions of the world. She imposed all of her fears and dysfunctional beliefs onto my young mind from a very early age. I grew up being scared of everything including the dark, the spirit world and the bad men (which apparently was every man) that 'were gonna get me'. So, I grew up consumed with fear and spent all my energies trying to be a 'good girl'. I figured if I was a good girl, I would be safe from bad men, evil spirits and what other people thought of me. But more importantly, I would be safe from disappointing my mother. She was a very loving and caring woman, but was the result of her own dysfunctional upbringing. My grandmother was a loving, saint-like, religious woman. All my memories are of her whispering prayers with rosary beads in hand.

While I never felt unloved by my parents or family, I learnt in my healing journey as an adult, that I had been emotionally neglected as a child. So, that combined with the fear-based beliefs and perceptions embedded deep within my psyche, I grew up in a state of total disempowerment. As a teenager I lacked confidence in my abilities, my looks, my intelligence and my power. I consciously dressed down so as not to attract the 'wrong' attention from males. Social gatherings were a constant source of angst. I became a master chameleon and could melt into a crowd and blend into my environment to become (in my mind) 'invisible'. I became fluent in accommodating others and their needs, ensuring my needs did not attract any attention.

This led to me adapting to role-playing on a constant and daily basis. I could be whoever or whatever was needed in the moment if it distracted attention away from me. The innate giver/nurturer in me excelled, and I began a long journey of habitually serving others needs and expectations, while neglecting my own. Subconsciously I was still being driven by the little good girl in me; not wanting to disappoint, fearful of rejection and longing for emotional acceptance and nurturing. This was to play out for the next 30 odd years of my life.

I met my now ex-husband at 17 years of age. I was married and had my first beautiful daughter, Ciara, a week after my 21st birthday. She was soon joined by my beautiful daughters Katie and Rhiannan, and my handsome son, Connor. I currently have seven gorgeous grandchildren who are the light of my heart.

As a wife and mother, I felt like I had finally found roles to which I could devote my energies. Still controlled by my subconscious drivers, I gave it my all and devoted every waking moment to being the best wife and mother I could be. And while I finally felt the love I had longed for - it slowly but surely became apparent that I was still compromising my own needs. My husband had been diagnosed with bipolar disorder which was compounded by alcohol abuse. Unfortunately, he refused the diagnosis and medication. Life became a rollercoaster of emotional, mental, and financial stress and drama. This soon took a toll on my physical health. By the time my four children had grown into young teenagers I began to experience anxiety attacks. I spent the best part of 12 months confined to my home, unable to drive or go out on my own. My husband was working away - which only added fuel to the ever-present stress levels. Many a night was spent in full anxiety attack mode, while my children slept. I applied every energy technique that I knew to survive the night. But on a few occasions, I had to succumb to dialling 000. After numerous ambulances trips, hospital stays, countless medical tests with no results or answers, I engaged a Naturopath to help me. The stress of my relationship had burned out my adrenals, my nervous and digestive systems and taken me below my healthy weight range. Twelve months and lots and lots of supplements later, my anxiety attacks became manageable.

So again, driven by my disempowering mindset of serving others needs before of my own, I spent the next few years trying to 'save' my husband. I was a Reiki Master and NLP Practitioner and had started my bachelor's degree in Metaphysical Sciences by then. I believed I had the tools and resources to make a difference. Naively I thought if I could save him it would save our marriage. This situation exposed all my deep held fears, and they were fully exposed in all their rawness. I had been a good girl, a good daughter, a good wife, a good mother and yet my world was crumbling. I could feel my soul withering away.

I spent many nights in my backyard crying to the stars and the universe asking 'Why?', 'What had I done wrong?', 'What else could I do?', 'What was the point and purpose of this situation?' I felt betrayed by life, by love and by my own inability to 'control' the situation. I contemplated many unsavoury options to escape but could never bear the thought of abandoning my children. They were the reason I stayed in body and spirit.

So, I was now faced with the biggest decision of my life. I felt like my soul was dying and I would have to muster all my courage to save it. A lifetime of fear-based perceptions, beliefs and existence were now more apparent than ever. I had never felt so alone and disempowered in all my life.

I remember crying to the stars and the universe on a beautiful clear night - telling the universe that I surrendered, that I had no more fight left in me. I was tired. My soul was tired. I consciously chose to let go and drop my need to control. In that moment, I gave up the fight and decided that it was too big for me. I humbly handed my future over into the care of the grace and wisdom of my soul. I had no choice but to trust that I would be supported and guided.

And this was my turning point.

I had been living my whole life from the mindset of being a victim; a victim to fear, a victim to avoiding rejection, a victim to the need of been accepted, a victim to other's opinions of me, a victim to pleasing others, a victim to fulfilling the roles required of me, a victim of my own internal controls driven by fear. I

had never made a single decision coming from a place of power. It was in this moment of surrender that a window of change and opportunity appeared.

'For things to change, first I must change'- Buckminster Fuller.

By letting go of the controls I gave myself the chance to be free from the structure of victimhood that had entrapped me all my life. It was the catalyst for the change that would ultimately lead me to connecting with my own power and Feminessence®.

From victim to victor mode and mindset.

In the lead up to leaving my marriage and home I told the stars and the universe what

I would need. I confidently placed my request of what I would require. By now I had started to really embrace this new way of being. I had been pushed to a place of survival and my innate Feminessence® instincts had started to kick in. So, I requested a unit by the beach, at an affordable price (under the laws of harmony and grace) that would accommodate me and my two teenage children who still lived with me. That request was heard and acted upon. I found a newly refurbished unit across the road from the beach, at a perfect price with an amazing landlord, and even more beautiful views. Coincidentally, this is the same place that I used to run away to. I would park at this beach and sleep in my car when things became too much for me at home. This alone cemented my confidence in my choice to create change and embody my power. My next request was for employment within ten minutes' drive along the same coastline. A week later I found the perfect job that sustained me, my children and our new lifestyle.

I had not only survived this major life change but had transitioned with ease and grace, all because I had chosen to connect to, embody and embrace my personal power and essence. I had claimed my self-worth and allowed myself to attend to my needs and those of my soul. I still remember the feeling of being invincible, victorious, and totally empowered. When I finally left my marriage, I told my husband that I loved him, but I loved me more.

Of course, not everyone shared my joy and enthusiasm. I had broken the mould of who I had been all my life. I had shattered the perceptions others had of me, and it was not received well by all. Sadly, it was those dearest and nearest to me that had the most conflict with my new-found sense of personal power. I was no longer playing the powerless victim. I was no longer accommodating others' needs and expectations. I had broken the unseen karmic promises, vows, and contracts. The people that I thought would support my new-found freedom and empowerment, unfortunately had their own agendas - even though they had witnessed the stress and drama I had endured for years. My fear of rejection had obviously survived my transition into the new empowered version of me. I had stepped into my soul's wisdom and strength, but some wounds still lingered.

I had dimmed my light all my life for the comfort of others. Suddenly, my light was able to shine freely but it was still hindered. I needed more soul-searching, more energy work, I needed to dig deeper into the depths of my internal stories. Feeling betrayed, disillusioned, and disappointed, I continued to delve into my subconscious programs, beliefs, and perceptions. I was determined to heal, clear, and recode anything that was stopping me from fully embodying all my true Feminessence® in all its beauty and glory.

So, once again I found myself letting go, surrendering, trusting that I just had to get out of the way. I decided to make peace with the past and began the process of forgiveness. I forgave those that I perceived were holding me in judgement. I forgave my husband for what I perceived he was guilty of. In fact, I thanked his soul for playing his karmic part in our story. If he had not played the 'bad' guy, I would never have connected with my Feminessence® power. And lastly, I forgave myself, for thinking that I had failed, that I had not done or tried enough; for thinking that I had being selfish in breaking up my family unit; for thinking that I had failed my children in some way and destroyed their future family dynamics. I forgave, I released, I detached from everything and everyone that was not supportive of my highest good. By embodying compassion, my world became smaller and quieter, but so much more peaceful. I began to build my new life knowing that it could only get better now that I was soulfully empowered.

I now had space in my head, my heart and soul to return to the one thing that had always been constantly burning in the background. My soul's passion and purpose were always to be a successful alternative healing therapist. As a child, I wanted to be a doctor, but as an adult I realised that holistic medicine was the path I would take. Taking a leap of faith, I enrolled for my Doctorate in Metaphysical Science - not quite a traditional medical doctor but I felt the need

for this level of training - as a commitment to myself and my chosen path. I didn't want to be just another healer. If I was going to make this my career I wanted to be taken seriously. So, I worked by day and studied every chance I had. I have now attained my bachelor's degree and I'm one dissertation and one thesis away from my Doctorate. I have added a few more modalities to my toolbox and feel that the learning is complete for now.

The last piece of my full Feminessence® empowerment came when I had to surrender yet again to my soul's knowing. I had been working full time in the hospitality sector and my healing business became a part-time gig. I once again felt my soul beginning to wither. I knew I wasn't doing what I was supposed to be doing, and I wasn't where I was supposed to be. But for financial reasons I was committed to working in a regular day job. My clientele began to dry up as I wasn't putting energy into my business. I could see the results I was creating by not fuelling my creative expression. I was not supporting my needs yet again and I could feel the old fear-based structures kicking in. More contemplation, more soul searching followed. Then it came to me. I had been in survival mode since I had left my marriage. It was another turning point for me, another layer of fear had been exposed. With this came even more commitment to creating the path to my calling; to being of service in helping others to connect with their own power and Feminessence®.

By now I had done a lot of healing on my core wounds and I had developed a healthy sense of my value and worth in the world. I had left my last two jobs feeling that I wasn't been valued. I was no longer prepared to compromise myself by accommodating others. I didn't play that game anymore.

My last and final position as an employee was the one that finally propelled me onto the path that I had longed for all my life. Again, I had to surrender and trust my Feminessence® power deeper than ever before. Leaving that position felt like stepping off the apex of the highest mountain into the darkness of the unknown. I left on a whim, with no plan, no back up, except for the love and support of my beautiful beloved soul partner, Steve. I spent the next 12 months creating and building the foundations of my healing practice. The path has been a constant flow of ease and grace. People, resources, and support seem to appear perfectly in each moment as needed. There is no more fear, doubt or resistance, just one perfect moment flowing onto the next.

This to me is the magic and power of feminine energy:

To be in total trust of Self. To honour and recognise the innate wisdom within. To give permission for that essence to manifest in every moment, situation, interaction and communication. To embody that power without fear, without resistance, without judgment, without limitation, without conditions. But most importantly, I believe the foundation of Feminessence® is letting go of the controls of 'needing to know'. A woman has an innate intuitive knowing, a sacred communication that can't be explained. By trusting in this inner communication, she becomes one with all that is.

This is Feminessence® in action.

Most men are not connected to that internal communication. Not that it's not available to them, it's just not in their hard drive. They are by nature bound to rational thinking. They are vertical in their logic, mechanically minded and not many live out their lives through intuition. They just use different software than women. No better, no less, simply different. They are in my opinion victims of social conditioning and pressures beyond their control. But I have no doubt that the tides of evolution are turning. The sacred feminine is rising globally and the balance will return. It is part of the human evolution and one day all humans will embody the male and female aspects in perfect harmony and unity.

I believe the integration has already begun as evident by current world events within social, government, educational and employment sectors. Eventually women will begin to balance out the numbers in all these sectors. I am confident that with the input of the feminine essence within all structures of society, the world will finally be able to benefit from that intuitive wisdom. They will imbue the systems with the nurturing and empathic qualities that only a woman can bestow. Maybe then the world will have that ease, grace and flow that is currently missing.

So, for now I continue to grow and expand my own business. I offer services that help my clients to discover their core wounds (from this life experience or others). My purpose and passion are to free them from anything that hinders their true essence. I know how it feels to be trapped in the victim structure and be disempowered; to feel like life is beyond your control. I believe everyone is capable and worthy of living their life from a place of empowerment and grace. I currently offer services that recode the physical, mental (subconscious) and soul's blueprint. In other words, I have the tools to provide healing in any area of the human experience. Wherever the imbalance is manifested, it can be recalibrated to the original blueprint of harmony and flow. I specialise in emotional healing, especially with women that have experienced victimisation in the past, (in this or other lifetimes) and help them to express their Feminessence® powers and gifts. I'm talking about empaths, healers, goddesses, gifted in the arts of healing and magic. I, myself have relived many past life memories of persecution, torture and condemnation for my feminine powers and skills. I always get great feedback from my clients because my intention is to over deliver results and value. I approach my clients and my work with soulful integrity and consider it an honour to share sacred space with them. I appreciate that they trust me with their deepest wounds and raw vulnerability.

I love what I do and I'm very grateful for the opportunity to be of service.

I offer sessions in energy healing, subconscious reprogramming, bioenergetic scanning of the human biofield, soul level coaching, successful mindset coaching, creating empowered outcomes, self-development and meditation. I will soon be offering online courses and workshops. All my offerings are provided in person or online and can be accessed as single sessions or in packages. I cater to all levels of awareness and all services are tailored to my client's needs.

My goal is to provide awareness and education around 'self-care and maintenance of the soul'. My agenda is to empower others to become soulfully and energetically self-sufficient, and completely empowered to create their desired reality and life experience with ease and grace. I don't want my clients to keep coming back forever. If they did, I would consider myself a failure. I want everyone to live a life they absolutely love, from a place of Love, Light and Power. Imagine how beautiful the world would be, if we were all living our own version of heaven on earth?

I choose to heal the world, one soul at a time.

OM SHANTI

*"From the centre, which we call the human race,
Let the Plan of Love and Light workout.
Let Light and Love and Power Restore the
Plan on Earth!"*

(Excerpt from the Great Invocation).

CAROL ARAVENA

Diamond-Light

M: 0427 106 009
E: quantumtransformations@hotmail.com
W: www.diamond-light.com

Carol has always had an awareness of spiritual energy. From a young age she experienced communication from behind the veil. After a chilling experience with a lost soul within the walls of her daughters' bedroom, her healing gifts began to surface. This experience started the journey of discovering and developing her innate gifts, and a lifelong fascination and interest with anything related to the unseen worlds.

After becoming a certified Reiki Master, she established a home-based natural therapy clinic. Further certification in NLP and colour therapy followed - by this stage there was no doubt that her future lay in the field of Metaphysics.

The interconnectedness of the human energy field and the subconscious were beginning to create a foundation for profound transformation in her clients. Carol became aware of the power of combining ancient healing modalities with modern science-based quantum therapies. Enrolling in her Doctorate in Metaphysical Sciences further expanded her knowledge, and her calling as a Metaphysical Practitioner was cemented. The importance of subconscious programs and perceptive constructs within the human consciousness have been her biggest learning and her strongest asset. This has been further supported with her certification as a Magnetic Mind Method Coach.

Carol believes that by clearing limiting subconscious beliefs, stories and programs, it is possible for anyone to create change. When combined with soul level energy healing, the client can then experience their life and reality from a place of empowerment and conscious choice. Moving them from a victim to a victor mindset.

Activity

The following process can be used to unpack some internal belief structures and expose the self-sabotage that is holding you back from having what you want.

1. What do you want to have, experience, or witness in your life that eludes you no matter how hard you try? Something that you just want, for no reason except that it feels good when you think about having it. Close your eyes. Now go ahead and see, feel, sense, experience and imagine yourself having it now, and really embody the emotions it brings.

Examples: money, love, health, vitality, peace, joy, purpose, empowerment, fulfillment.

____

____

____

2. Now come back to the present and notice where you are now in relation to what you want. How far away is the thing you want? On a scale from 1-10 where are you now compared to where you want to be? (1 being close to, 10 being away from)

____

____

____

3. Why do YOU think you can't have that now?

Make a list of all the reasons you can think of - no matter how small, silly or insignificant. Let the stories roll out. Let yourself go inwards and just listen without judgment or attachment.

____

____

____

4. Now look at your list of reasons and with each one I want you to ask yourself these two questions-

'What would a person have to believe for that reason to be true?'

'What lets me know this belief is true?'

Keep asking and delving inwards. Eventually you will begin to see a pattern of recurring beliefs. They will generally correspond with and fall into one of the following self-sabotaging personalities.

1. I am unlovable
2. I am not worthy
3. I am insignificant
4. I am not good enough
5. I am not smart enough
6. I am not accepted

These self-sabotaging aspects of your personality are stopping you from having what you desire. Heal your wounding to heal your story, and create a life you love.

OFFER:

As a special for Feminessence® Readers

I am offering the first 20 readers that enrol for 6 months of Transformational Coaching with me the following bonuses:
FREE access to the Magnetic Mind Masterclass course via the self-paced online University (worth over $2300)
Access to the private Magnetic Mind Masterclass Facebook group
Access to over 20 MP3 meditations to empower your transformation journey.